Marketing Untangled Series

Marketing Communications Untangled

The Small Business & Entrepreneur's Guide to Choosing the Right Marketing Communications

By

Thoranna Jonsdottir

Already available in the series:

Marketing Untangled: *The Small Business & Entrepreneur's Map Through the Marketing Jungle*

Target Groups Untangled: *The Small Business & Entrepreneur's Guide to Finding and Knowing Your Ideal Target Groups*

Competition Untangled: *The Small Business & Entrepreneur's Guide to Knowing Your Competition*

Branding Untangled: *The Small Business & Entrepreneur's Guide to Building Your Brand*

Coming Up in The Series: *Make sure you don't miss it by signing up at thoranna.is/marketinguntangledseries*

Marketing Systems Untangled: *The Small Business & Entrepreneur's Guide to Setting Up an Effective Marketing System*

Dedication

For Kalli, Ísold Saga, and Ísak Máni,
who support me in whatever I do.

Contents

The Marketing Untangled Series – Why I Wrote It and How It Works!. 1

Read This First: On Marketing Communications 9

Part I 15

   1. Choose the Right Ways to Communicate. 17

   2. The Marketing Process. 25

   3. Lead Management 41

   4. Lead Them 57

   5. Measure 61

Part II 63

Marketing Activities. 65

   Priority 1: Marketing Activities You Must Use. 69

   Priority 2: Marketing Activities You Must Use but Not Until After Priority 1! 89

   Priority 3: Marketing Activities You May Want to Use A Few More Ideas. 107

   A Few More Ideas. 133

   Social Media. 165

Building Your Marketing Communications Program 181

About the Author 187

Endnotes 189

Further References 191

Acknowledgements

There are a few people who I would like to thank.

My husband and children are always going to be at the top of my list, as well as my parents, little brother, and sister-in-law. I appreciate their unwavering support for everything I do and their patience when I get yet another idea and always strive for more. As we say in my house, "When Mom is happy, everyone is happy." That's just how it is. :) My family's endless belief in me, even as I lose faith in myself, is an endless source of strength, as is their support as I continue to seek even more ways to be the best I can be.

My clients throughout the years deserve a big thank you for appreciating what I know and do and for acting on it. Seeing you use what I have taught you and getting results with it is the reason I do this. It's the reason I am getting these books out, even though life has gotten in the way, and my journey has developed and changed since I first began working on the training program that is the basis of these books.

Endless thanks to my Runa, who always reminds be to be just who I am and that I am enough. When many others want me to be more sterile and boring to be "professional," she reminds me that there is only one me and that is a gift. Being professional is not the same as being boring. You can be professional and competent and still have fun and enjoy life! And boy, do we enjoy it when we're together.

Thank you, Mummi, for helping make this vibrant pink marketing nerd look good.

I have been blessed with a lot of good people in my life who have inspired and supported me. The list would be too long ... you know who you are, and you know I love you. However, I do want to mention a few key clients throughout the years who have meant the world to me and have become dear friends—people such as Davíð, Dóri, Martha, Herdís, Heiðrún, Katrín, Rut, Ingvar, Jóhann Friðrik, and many more who prove to me how awesome it can be to work with great people!

The Marketing Untangled Series - Why I Wrote It and How It Works!

Through all my years of working in marketing—whether at agencies, within businesses, or as a consultant, teacher, or mentor—things always come back to the same basic foundational things again and again. People are anxious to see results and, therefore, tend to want to dive into tactics—what advertising to do, which social media to be on, what to say, and so on. Well, here's the truth of the matter: tactical decisions in marketing cannot be made without a solid strategy—a rock-solid foundation. This is why, without exception, I have always had to bring my clients and students back to the foundation, the marketing strategy. These foundations will then tell you what marketing tactics to use, which channels are best, and what you should say in your marketing messages; your marketing communications. I have also found that marketing is as much about organisation, research, and project management as it is about strategy and tactics. Without this underlying backbone of organisation and planning, your efforts will be unfocused, inconsistent, and sporadic, which is not conducive to good results.

This is why I developed materials and processes to lead my clients and students through, allowing them to build a solid marketing strategy and program that works—to build a system for your marketing, a marketing machine, that you can run to get the customers and business you want. I call it my map through the marketing jungle—my step-by-step process for untangling the marketing mess (hence *Marketing Untangled*).

It consists of five steps, and each of these steps are the subject of a separate book in the *Marketing Untangled* series, as well as the topics covered in the modules of my online training program, *The Marketing Untangled Training*.

I'm not going to pretend that I came up with all this myself. I didn't. These things have been researched, studied, tried, and tested in business and academia around the world. The strategies are the same ones underlying the success of businesses we see all around us: Apple, Coca-Cola, Nike, but also thousands of small- and medium-sized businesses that have grown to where they want to be and perhaps did not want to become the next global corporation. What I have done is distil all this knowledge and experience into a practical, jargon-free, step-by-step process suitable to the needs of entrepreneurs and small and medium businesses. What you need to know, nothing more—and nothing less—in an easy to digest and easy to use manner—no fluff, no academic mumbo jumbo.

The purpose of these books is not to make you a marketing expert, nor should you necessarily want to be one. However, if you own or run a business, you must have a good understanding of marketing.

Why? Because marketing is at the heart of business. Marketing is your business. It is the lifeblood of your business. Marketing is what gets customers; without customers, you don't have a business. It is all about understanding the needs of the customers and fulfilling those in a profitable way; that is the definition of marketing. As Al Ries said, *"Marketing is what a company is in business to do. Marketing is a company's ultimate objective."*[1]

Peter Drucker had it spot on: *"Marketing is the distinguishing, the unique function of the business ... Marketing is not only much broader than selling, it is not a specialized activity at all. It is the whole business seen from the point of view of the final result, that is from the customer's point of view.*

Concern and responsibility for marketing must, therefore, permeate all areas of the enterprise."[2]

I'd ask whether you still think marketing has nothing to do with you—but then, you'd probably not be reading this book. ;)

The other reason for having a good understanding of marketing strategy and the various marketing communications options is because when you do buy marketing services or hire marketing staff, you need to be an informed buyer. You may not want to become an expert in social media or search engine optimisation or any of the other tools and tactics available to you, but you should have a basic understanding of what they are and what they are supposed to do so you know what services you are buying, what skills you are hiring, and whether they are working for you.

Since my life as a marketing nerd started at the dawn of this new century, I have seen far too many great businesses fail to reach their potential, and many fail completely. I have seen entrepreneurs with an incredible amount of passion for what they do get absolutely nowhere. I have seen fantastic products and services fall by the wayside. In the majority of those cases, it is because the team lacked understanding of and skills in marketing. A 2012 literary review at the University of Iceland showed without a shadow of a doubt that marketing orientation (looking at business from the point of view of the customer *à la* Drucker) and marketing skills are the single biggest business success factors, irrespective of business size.[3] This is simply something people cannot ignore, and, if left unattended, your business will curl up and die.

However, we can't all become marketing experts, and we can't all spend years getting marketing degrees (and many would argue their limited usability in the marketing trenches, anyway). We need the most effective injection of marketing knowledge and understanding possible, and that is exactly what *Marketing Untangled* is all about and exactly what I want to give you.

This book is about that part of marketing that most want to jump straight into: marketing communications. It covers what tools, tactics, and communication channels to use. It helps you answer common questions: should you advertise here or there, should you be on Twitter or Snapchat or Quora, and should you do public speaking or hand out flyers. More often than not, this is the first thing people go to when they want to improve their marketing. However, jumping straight in here is like running to the hardware store, buying a hammer, nails, and a few planks of wood, thinking you will end up with the house of your dreams. We all know things don't work that way when building a house, and they don't work that way in marketing, either. You need to lay the groundwork and create a blueprint by building a well-thought-out marketing strategy.

Your strategy is extremely important and worth doing well, because it lays a solid foundation for all your marketing efforts and makes all your marketing activities much more focused and efficient. One could say that your strategy work is 80 percent of your marketing, so if you do your job well with this stuff, the other 20 percent will be so much more effective.

A solid marketing strategy also makes all your marketing decisions so much easier. It works a bit like a compass. When you are not sure what to do, you can go back to your strategy, and it will help you make a decision. If things fit within the strategy, you are off to the races; if not, you will have a clear reason why and be able to let that idea go without having to worry if it was the right thing.

There are three pillars to building your marketing strategy; then—and only then—will you have a powerful launchpad for your marketing communications: knowing your target groups, knowing your competitors, and based on these two, creating a strategy for the brand you want to build. These are the subjects of three previous books in the *Marketing Untangled* series: *Target Groups Untangled*, *Competition Untangled*, and *Branding Untangled*.

In *Target Groups Untangled*, I discussed the importance of knowing your audience, or your target groups. In that book, I showed how to determine your target groups and what you need to know and understand about them to be able to effectively reach them. This is the first element in building a strong marketing strategy.

The second marketing strategy pillar is knowing and analysing the competition. You need to know them because they represent other options your potential customers are considering. If you don't know them, you'll have an impossible task of explaining to people why they should choose your products and services, instead of what your competitors are offering. The competition, who they are, what you need to know about them, where you can find out about them, what to do with that information and how it can help you, were subjects of another book in the series, *Competition Untangled*.

One of the most important things knowledge of the competition gives you is that it allows you to differentiate yourself from them—to be able to confidently answer when someone asks, "Why should I buy from you rather than them?" That differentiation then becomes a core element in your brand, the third pillar of your marketing strategy, and the subject of *Branding Untangled*.

Your brand is the mental and emotional associations people have with you, your business, product, or service. In other words, your brand is what they think and feel about you—and make no mistake, this is arguably the single most important thing in marketing. Why? Because people buy based on thoughts and feelings, and your brand is what determines what they think of you, how they feel about you, and hence whether they buy from you. Also, having a strong and interesting brand, being different and distinctive from the competition, is an absolute necessity to cut through the noise of a crowded marketplace and get noticed. In *Branding Untangled*, I lead you through the strategy for successfully building a brand, deciding what you want people to think and feel about you, and how you can build that brand in the hearts and minds of the people.

Once you have those solid foundations for your marketing strategy, then, and only then, can you start thinking about what marketing communications channels, tools, and tactics to use and what to say to your market. Your target groups will tell you where you can reach them and what marketing messages will be most effective, and your brand (which needs to be different and distinctive from the competition) will help you get noticed and get people's attention.

In this book, *Marketing Communications Untangled*, we look at the fourth part of the process: your marketing communications and how everything you do needs to support each other and create a holistic program to get people to buy from you. People don't just see your ad once and jump straight into buying. You need to make sure you have the right tools to attract them and get them to buy, so your selection of marketing communications tools and how to make everything work together in a systematic fashion is vitally important. I also introduce and place at your disposal a multitude of marketing communications tools and tactics and give you guidelines to help you choose those that are right for your business.

The final part of an effective marketing program is setting up a system. Knowing all about your target groups and competition, having a kick-ass brand strategy, knowing exactly what you want to say in your marketing messages and what channels and tools you are going to use to get your message out there is useless if it doesn't actually get done. When you are running a start-up or small or medium business, it is easy to get distracted and not get your marketing done. This is deadly. The only way to get things done is by getting organised. This is covered in the final book in the series, *Marketing Systems Untangled*. It's all about getting your marketing organised, taking all the work you did on strategy and marketing communications and using that as a "springboard" to set up a plan—finalising that map through the marketing jungle so you can then start to follow it step-by-step to your money tree.

If the target groups, competition, and brand are the pillars of the launchpad for your marketing communications rocket, then the marketing system is the fuel that makes sure it actually gets off the platform and keeps soaring!

As you can see, although I've broken the process into five steps and five separate books, these elements do not work in isolation. They all need to come together to form a marketing strategy and program that works and gets you customers. I, therefore, encourage you to read the other books in the series and use them to put your marketing machine together. To further help you gain an overview of the five parts of the

Marketing Untangled series, I would like to give you a free copy of the first and original book, *Marketing Untangled: The Small Business & Entrepreneur's Map Through the Marketing Jungle.* This book acts as an introduction to the series and gives you a more detailed overview of the five elements of the process and how they fit together. You will find your copy in the reader resources for this book at thoranna.is/mcureader. Get in there now to create your account and get your free access!

One final thing: things do not happen by themselves. In order for the materials in this book to actually be helpful, they must be put to use. It is not enough to just read it. I suggest you open your calendar or diary and set aside time to regularly work on your marketing, whether it is working through this book or any other marketing activities that need to be done. More often than not, it is not the cleverest individuals in the world who achieve success, but rather the ones who take action. Knowledge is not power unless it informs action. And the fact is most people simply don't act; they simply don't do. Don't be one of them. Take action!

Okay, I won't keep you any longer. Let's dive into this marketing communications thing, shall we. Here we go...

Read This First: On Marketing Communications

"Because the purpose of business is to create a customer, the business enterprise has two—and only two—basic functions: marketing and innovation. Marketing and innovation produce results; all the rest are costs. Marketing is the distinguishing, unique function of the business."

— Peter Drucker[4]

Marketing is the lifeblood of your business. Without it, you will have no customers ... and without customers, you have no business.

When most non-specialists think of marketing, they are really thinking of marketing communications. Often, people don't realise how much the concept of marketing encompasses. In the image below, you can see some of it, but this is by no means exhaustive.

As you can see, marketing communications is just one part of what marketing encompasses—an important part, for sure, but only a part.

Within marketing communications, you then have a range of disciplines, which I will not exhaustively list, either, but just to give you an idea:

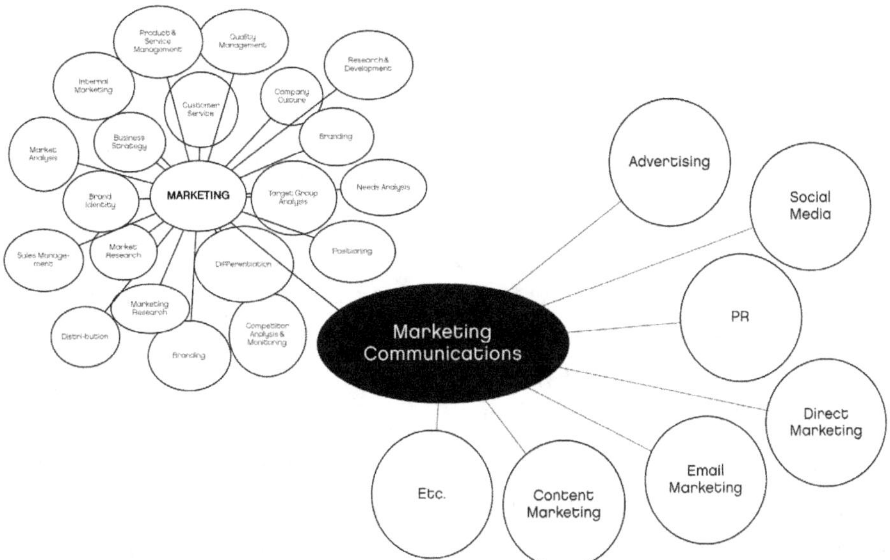

It is, therefore, extremely important not to look at marketing communications in isolation, but as one part of the whole, which is influenced by all other parts of marketing. In classic marketing texts, you will often see a discussion about the "marketing mix." The marketing mix, the components of marketing you have to play with to create a marketing program, originally consisted of 4 Ps, which stood for:

- Product (or service)
- Place (location and distribution)
- Price
- Promotion (marketing communications, or marcoms for short)

But as the world becomes more complicated, people have added Ps. There are Ps such as:

- People
- Packaging
- Positioning

- Process
- Physical environment
- Physical evidence
- Productivity
- Payment

And there are probably a few floating out there that I haven't included. As you can see, people have managed to find a lot of Ps! So many in fact, that this whole concept of the Ps in the marketing mix is ceasing to be useful. For that reason, I won't be approaching marcoms based on the marketing mix. What we are focusing on here mainly falls under the "Promotion P." What is important to keep in mind, though, is that whichever way you look at it, Ps or no Ps, everything that lives under this umbrella of "marketing" interlinks and influences each other. If you change the packaging, that may mean having to raise the price—or it can be more cost effective so that you can lower it (Ikea is a great example of where packaging is a great influence on price, and they have done some amazing things in their designs to accomplish cost savings and thereby lower prices). If you change the place (location) to one with lower footfall, you need to increase your promotion to get people in. That works in cyberspace, as well. You will need to do a lot more promotional work to drive traffic to your own standalone website to sell your products than if you sell them in a virtual "mall" like Amazon or eBay, where people are already looking for things (in reality, Amazon and eBay are simply large product search engines). If you strip down the product, you can lower prices (think no-frills airlines) and so on and so forth.

The point I want to make is that this book in isolation is not enough. It will tell you a lot of things that you need to know when it comes to marketing communications, and it will give you a wide array of options from which to choose. But you need to look at this all in the context of your marketing strategy and all the other things you are doing within your business.

With regards to your strategy, there are three major things in your strategy that influence your choice of marketing communications. Your target groups and your brand are two of them. I will discuss both of these briefly, but if you are not 100 percent clear on your target groups and don't have a solid brand strategy, I suggest you check out other books in the *Marketing Untangled* series, specifically *Target Groups Untangled* and *Branding Untangled*, for more in-depth information about both of these things. You can find information about them in the reader resources for this book at thoranna.is/mcureader. The third thing is building a lead management system that will move people through the marketing process, from the first time they become aware of you, until the sale and beyond. We will be discussing that in detail. The fourth and final major thing influencing your choice of marketing activities is you, and your business, which we will discuss, as well.

One final point before we get going on those marketing activities: it is one thing to have a clear strategy, and know which marketing activities you should be using, and another thing to get results. Knowledge without action will get you nowhere. After running my own small businesses and having worked with hundreds of small business owners and entrepreneurs, I have found that the magic bullet is a combination of action and organisation. Therefore, the final book in the *Marketing Untangled* series is about marketing systems—not the software kind, but the project management kind. The book discusses the kind of systems and organisation that help us get our marketing activities done and help us consistently keep at it. The action part, you then have to bring to the table ;) *Marketing Systems Untangled: The Small Business & Entrepreneur's Map to Setting Up an Effective Marketing System* will be out soon to help you with the organisation bit. ;)

Here is what we will be covering in this book about marketing communications:

- We will briefly discuss the subject of target groups, as we need to make sure we are using the right channels to reach the people we want to reach and have the right message to attract them. For a more detailed discussion, please refer to *Target Groups Untangled.*

- This book also briefly discusses brand and branding and how it influences your decisions about marketing communications. Without a clear brand strategy, your marketing communications will not be focused, and you will not be able to unlock their capabilities (I would say you can only get about 20 percent out of them, whereas if you add solid knowledge of your target groups and a brand strategy that builds a brand that appeals to them, you will add the other 80 percent and then some!). For a more detailed discussion on branding, please refer to *Branding Untangled.*

- We will go through the marketing process, which is the process we must lead people through in order to make the sale and continue our relationship with them.

- We will then go over building a lead management system, which allows us to choose the right marketing communications and communications tools to help us lead people through the marketing process.

- We will discuss how we need to lead people from one point to the next and measure the results of our efforts at each of these points.

- We will go over a substantial list of marketing communications options, categorised by priority.

You will then be able to get even more information, insights, and resources in the reader resources for the book at thoranna.is/mcureader.

Let's start with discussing the four things that should influence your choice of marcoms.

PART I

1. Choose the Right Ways to Communicate

Only when you are clear on your target market and the brand you want to build, can you begin choosing the marketing activities to construct that brand and communicate with your audience. Should you be on Twitter, advertise in this magazine or that newspaper, or send out flyers? Whatever you do must be determined by four things:

- Your target groups
- Your brand
- Yourself
- And creating a system that leads to the sale and beyond

Your Target Groups

It seems straightforward enough, doesn't it? Be where you can reach your target audience. Are they on Facebook? What newspapers do they read or which magazines? Do they go to conferences? Which ones? It is very important to know these things about your target group so you can reach them where they are and where they are open to receiving your message. It's not just about where to reach them, but also how to reach them. How to actually make them sit up, listen, and take action. What message will be most effective? How should you present that message, etc.?

In order to best be able to do this, you need to have:

- Identified and defined your target groups, whether they are in B2B (business-to-business) or B2C (business-to-consumer) markets and decided which ones you should be focusing on first. You can't effectively reach everyone at the same time, so you need to prioritise and focus your efforts. Don't try to conquer the world all at once (but do conquer it, even if it's just your own little corner of it ;)).

- Organised your target groups to see which products or services you should be offering to which groups. I suggest mapping your products and services in relation to your groups and vice versa. This will help organise the targeting of your communications. We wouldn't want one big mess, because that will get us nowhere.

- Gotten to know and understand as much as possible about your target groups, so that you know what marketing messages will resonate most effectively with them and where to best reach them. Just knowing demographics like age and gender does not do you much good in today's crowded and complicated world and fragmented media, be it online or offline. You need to understand what drives them, what their needs and problems are, hence, their reasons to buy, and what it is that matters to them the most in their choices of what they buy and who from.

If you are not crystal clear on your target groups, you may want to check out *Target Groups Untangled: The Small Business & Entrepreneur's Guide to Knowing and Finding Target Groups*. You can find more information about it in the reader resources at thoranna.is/mcureader.

Your Brand

As the concept of the brand is not always clear, I want to start by briefly ensuring that we are on the same page: A brand is basically everything that people associate with you in their minds and hearts (whether "you" refers to you personally, your product, service, or business). When your brand is mentioned or people see something from you, something specific will come to their mind, even if they have never heard or seen your brand before. Think about it; think of any word or name. Something will always come to your mind. There will always be an emotion attached to it. It may be weak, but it will be there. If I say "mellano," you immediately get some thoughts in your head. The psychological influence of colour is well known. What comes to mind when you see bright red? What about purple? See ... there are always some mental and emotional associations, no matter how little people see or hear of things, and you want to make sure that the associations people have with your brand will make them want to buy from you.

EXAMPLE: Santa

We all know Santa, whatever our religious and cultural background. Santa is a good example of a very strong brand. We all have the same mental associations, largely built by Coca-Cola since the 1930's, and most of us have positive emotions toward him. In the following image, you can see some of those universal mental and emotional associations.

Now consider this: We buy based on *feelings*. Research has shown this again and again. We are not *rational* beings; our feelings guide us. At some point, our brains take over and we usually rationalize our purchase, sometimes before and sometimes after. Your brand evokes thoughts and feelings, and those thoughts and feelings dictate whether people buy. Hence, it can be argued that *your brand is the single most important determinant of whether people buy from you or not!*

Upon hearing the word "brand", many people immediately think of logos and design, which is definitely part of a brand, just as the clothes people wear represent who they are as individuals. However, to say that a brand is *just* the logo and design is like saying a person is just her clothes, with nothing inside. A brand is the whole, the total being of your business, product, service, or you, as a small business owner or entrepreneur. It is the people's *experience* of *you*.

We all have a *brand*, whether we realise it or not. The mere mention of your business, product, or service will conjure up some mental and emotional associations. It is crucial we don't leave it up to luck to determine what those associations are. You must take an active role in creating your brand in the minds of consumers to ensure that it will attract them to you and get them to buy.

This leads me to another point: your brand is not what *you* say it is—it is what *they* say it is. Or as Jeff Bezos of Amazon fame is supposed to have so aptly put it, "*Your brand is what people say about you when you are not in the room.*"

What do you want people to say about *your* business, product, or service when you are not present?

The importance of your brand to your marketing cannot be overstated. Seth Godin is quoted in *Forbes* (2007) as saying:

"Often a small business will run into problems, when the owners don't take that time early on to understand and build their individualized brand ... Small

businesses become bigger when their marketing strikes a chord. They fail when they struggle to stay average ... if you build your brand right, you won't need to allocate more funds for marketing."[5]

I could not agree more. A strong brand is your most effective marketing tool; it will amplify the effect of everything else in your marketing—*all* your marketing activities.

A strong and distinctive brand ensures that you cut through the clutter, stand out from others in the marketplace, and have maximum impact on those you reach.

Marketing activities are a major part of what builds your brand; therefore, to start doing them without having defined the brand you want to build is folly. It is like building a house on sand. You will be stacking those bricks day in and day out, but instead of seeing walls rising and a house being built, the bricks just keep sinking into the sand and nothing ever gets up from the ground.

The very basic steps in building a brand are:

- Determining what your brand is today so you know where you are working from.
- Determining what you want your brand to be, bearing in mind...
  o The target audience you want to appeal to.
  o Your competition, because you want to be different from them to stand out in the market.
  o You and your business—you can't be something you are not.
- Building that brand by consistently communicating it through every possible touchpoint with your business, product, or service—of which your marketing communications are a large part.

The brand you want to build affects your choice of marketing activities. But, no less important, the environment in which you reach your target groups will affect your brand. It will affect how people see you and their feelings toward you. Make sure the mental and emotional connections they bring are positive. You may find media or places where you know your target audience hangs out, but do they fit *your* brand? Tabloids are a good example. They may have a large readership, but if you want your brand to be classy and sophisticated, you don't want the brand association that a tabloid ad may bring, just as you don't want to promote your specialist services on a silly gameshow. Similarly, do not place the same ad in a tabloid as the one you put in the *New York Times* or *The Guardian* or sell your classy jewellery in a sleazy part of town. Context matters. Make sure you want your brand to be seen in the context which your marketing activities give it.

The brand also greatly affects how you use those marketing activities. As an example, with a clear brand, it is much easier to know what to say and how to behave on social media if you know what kind of character your brand has and how you want to be experienced. Knowing how you want people to experience your brand serves as a compass for what you do in your marketing activities. What do you say and do on social media? What kind of language do you use in your marketing copy? What is your brand's personality? Are you funny? Wise? Cheeky? Respectable? Know what you want your brand to be, and you'll know how to behave. And remember to present yourself in the appropriate way for where you are. If you are on Facebook, be fun, interesting, and sociable. On LinkedIn, you can be a bit more serious and professional. But I must confess I hate when people think being likeable and fun means one is less professional or trustworthy. This is *not* the case; it only means we get a lot of boring, faceless, and heartless businesses.

For a deeper discussion on branding, and guidance on how to create and build your brand, refer to a previous book in the series, *Branding Untangled.*

What's Right for You?

If you are Coca Cola or Unilever, you can afford to just go for the marketing activities you want and are likely to be most effective. When those companies don't have the necessary knowledge and resources inhouse, they either hire in and buy stuff or outsource. But when you are an entrepreneur, startup, or small business, you usually don't have that luxury.

When choosing your marketing approach, think about whether you have the necessary knowledge and skills *within* the company; if you do, *use them*. Is there a good writer for that blog? Or someone who is photogenic and a good speaker who can do that video? Or another employee who knows how to edit them? Do you have the money to pay for outside help to teach you or your staff, or even do things for you? And if you can find someone to teach you or your staff, are any of you actually *interested* in learning?

Learning new things is great. The Internet means that a huge variety of courses and resources are at your fingertips, but you also have to be realistic as to how much time and energy you have. Sometimes the best thing is to get help from those who know how to do things. Examine your network. Do you know someone who can help you or teach you? If not, can you pay for it?

It may be that a certain activity is perfect for your market and your product / service, but if you don't have the knowledge, skills, and resources for it, go to the next best thing on the list. No less important, do you—or the individual within your business who will be performing the task—actually *enjoy* it? Because if you're not keen on writing a blog, you won't do a good job. If you hate being on Twitter, you are not going to get positive results, etc. *If it doesn't float your boat, don't do it!*

Lead Them to Water and Make Them Drink

The fourth thing you need in order to determine which marketing activities you should use is to ensure that you have what you need to effectively build a system that leads people toward buying from you and beyond. Folks need to go through a mental process before they are willing to buy from you; I simply call it "The Marketing Process." We then need to ensure we have the tools to move them through this process to get the sale; we need to build a system to manage your leads. A lead is a person who is *in* your marketing process; they are aware of you and interested in what you have to offer. You need to have a system in place to manage this person through the process—a lead management system. The next two chapters are devoted to these two things, the marketing process and your lead management system.

2. The Marketing Process

Before you can choose the right marketing communications activities for you, it is important to understand the marketing process. People need to go through a certain process before they are ready to buy from you. How long it takes depends on the product or service, marketing environment, and various other factors. What is important to remember is that marketing takes time.

Think about it in the same way as personal relationships. If you like someone, you don't just walk up to them and ask them to marry you, do you? No, you start slow. You introduce yourself, get to know them, find out what they are like, and what they like. And you feel your way forward. You will know when the right moment presents itself, when you feel that you can pop the question and are likely to get a positive answer. And you start with a small ask; a cup of coffee, a dinner date, meeting the parents—you don't just jump straight to the proposal! :) Marketing is just the same. People are not ready to buy from you as soon as they see you. You need to build that relationship.

It depends on which sources you cite, but it takes between 7 and 21 contacts with a brand before people are prepared to buy it. That's quite a lot! Always keep this in mind. Don't rush things. This is one of the reasons frequency and consistency are so important. With limited resources, it's more important to reach the right people a number of times than it is to reach a lot of people once or only a few times.

Patience is also very important in marketing, and you must repeat the same things over and over and over again. You constantly have to imprint your brand and your message in people's minds, wherever you can, and as often as you can to make sure it sticks in their heads. If they can't remember you, they are not likely to buy from you.

Incidentally, my clients sometimes complain that they get bored with their marketing. They are bored with saying the same things, looking the same, using the same colours, etc. I'll tell you what I tell them: "If you are doing the same things over and over again to the point that you are dying of boredom, that is fantastic! Great! That means you are doing it right." Remember that people out there will only see a tiny fragment of what you are doing in your marketing efforts. If you're lucky, they may see one percent of it. They are not bored. They have just barely noticed you. They have just barely started to remember you and understand what you are and what you do. If you keep changing things up, they will think they are seeing something new. To them, it will feel like the first point of contact.

Recently, I had a consultation with a successful educational institute in Iceland. One of the directors is a graphic designer, and she was itching to change their logo, and they were even considering a name change. They had moved to new and fantastic facilities and felt they should mark the occasion with a makeover. "Hang on...," I said, "things are going great, you can afford to now move into the facilities you have always dreamed of, and now you want to start changing things up." I managed to convince them that this was not a good idea. They have spent a lot of time and money building up awareness, getting their brand recognised and remembered. And they had just moved. Can you imagine what would have happened if at that point they would have also changed the name and the logo? They would have been back to square one when it comes to establishing themselves in the minds of their target audience.

I often liken this to a game of snakes and ladders. By constantly working on your marketing, you will gradually move up the board. Once in a while, you will hit something great, like getting major media exposure or having a very successful campaign, or something else that will get you up that ladder, giving you a shortcut up the board. But if you start changing things up, changing your message or the look of your brand, that snake will take you right back down again, sometimes as far as square one. I am not saying you should not finetune things, develop or take steps to ensure you don't become outdated, but don't make changes solely for the sake of it. This is one of those times when the creativity of an entrepreneur can be detrimental to a business. The only person who can tell you that you may need to make more than just small changes and finetuning to your brand identity and marketing is your financial director, when the sales start dropping— not you or someone close to your brand who wants change just for the sake of change. ;)

How long it takes people to go through the marketing process varies greatly, depending on your product or service. It may not take a long time to decide to buy a pack of chewing gum—it's cheap, there is low risk, and if you don't like it, you just won't buy it again. However, you do need to trust that there is nothing in it that is bad for you (some of us would put sugar in that category, others wouldn't, but you also literally have to trust basic things such as that it's not poisonous). When you buy a car, however, or when companies invest in expensive machinery or even large factories, the process can take a lot longer. The more expensive the purchase or the more personal it is, the longer it generally takes to get people to buy - the marketing process takes longer to go through.

Way back when, I was the co-founder of a company introducing cloud-based software-as-a-service to the Icelandic market. Not only were we very early in the innovation curve and had to educate the market about our services, but we also had to literally create the market as people simply didn't understand what it was. "The cloud?!" Even more challenging, those who did understand the service were more often than not locked into software contracts for months, even years. They may have wanted to jump straight into doing business with us, but they simply couldn't. This is a prime example where the marketing process took quite a long time.

You must ensure that you have effective activities for each stage of the marketing process. This will help move her through the process, toward purchase and beyond. This is the purpose of your marketing program. The process is outlined in the following image – take a good look and then let's go over each part in more detail:

AWARENESS

Before anything else, people need to simply be aware of your brand – they must know you exist. That is the first step, and often that is a marketing activity's only objective: to let people know you are there or remind them you are there, so they don't forget. Marketing is often used simply to be "top of mind" when people eventually need what you have to offer. You want to make sure you are the first thing that people think of when they need the sort of thing you are offering.

In order to get people's awareness, you need to be constantly visible, instantly recognisable, and you need to stand out from the crowd. Be different and more interesting than the others. Your brand is a crucial element in this, and this is also the main reason why you need to be consistent with your brand strategy and brand identity. If you change your brand identity, things such as colours or fonts, people will not recognise you and you will have to start to build awareness from scratch again – remember those snakes and ladders. In my previous life, as an actress, one of the things we were taught at drama school, and this was also something my agent emphasized, was to always wear the same clothes, same hairstyle, and the same kind of makeup to each audition for the same gig. This ensured that when you came in for your second or third (or later) audition, people would remember you more than if you suddenly turned up looking different from the auditions before. This is classic marketing: repeat, repeat, repeat...

A few examples of marketing communications tools that can create awareness are advertising, social media statuses that spread virally, content that spreads virally (e.g. blog posts, videos, infographics), and media coverage.

INTEREST

However, once you're on people's radar, it is not enough for them to know you exist. They may not have any need for what you have to offer, and even if they do, they may not realise it. For example, I may notice an ad for Caterpillar diggers, but I have absolutely no need for them whatsoever, so I will not move any further in the process. Or people may notice you and not really like what they see. In any case, if you don't get people's interest, the process stops there. You need to get them interested and wanting to know more about you.

Once you've piqued their interest, you need to reel them in and get them to join you wherever possible, be that following you on social media, reading your blog, looking at your website—not to mention signing up for your email list.

People won't buy what they are not interested in. People even prefer one brand of chewing gum over another simply because something about it got them more interested in that one. Even the tiniest difference in interest can make a difference – so be interesting! A purple cow is bound to be a lot more interesting than the usual black and white one (as Seth Godin explains in his great little book *Purple Cow*[6]). How is your brand interesting? How is what you say in your marketing communications interesting? How can you be visually interesting? Knowing your target groups and what would interest them is, therefore, crucial, and a strong brand can be the difference between grabbing people's interest or being ignored.

"But my product / service is not interesting," you may say. I say, "Bull!" Anything can be interesting; and if you doubt me, may I introduce the fabulous brand that is Poo-Pourri. Huge players in the fast-moving consumer-goods market have for decades sold spray cans with chemicals designed to mask the stink of your no. 2. You may have bought some at some point, but I doubt that you have a particular brand preference in that category. They're all pretty much the same. Some have pink flowers, others have yellow lemons; that's about the extent of their variety. In 2013, Poo-Pourri set the Internet on fire with their hilarious video entitled "Girls' Don't

Poop," where a very posh woman with a British accent told the viewer all about her no. 2s and Poo-Pourri.[7] They used fantastic branding—not in the least brilliant use of language—to make a product as boring, unappealing, and uninteresting as poo spray a fantastic hit. They had rave reviews on Amazon (who reviews poo spray on Amazon! Lol!) and, according to their website, the video increased their website traffic by 13,000 percent![8] You really have to see this, so I've put links to my Pinterest collection of Poo-Pourri in the reader resources at thoranna.is/mcureader. This really is proof of the power of creative and fun branding!

The same tools that can be used for awareness need to be used for this. Awareness without interest is useless to you. Your brand and brand identity are crucial at this stage. Also note, it is not until both of these stages of the process have passed that a lot of core marketing tools come into play, like your website and your mailing list. People won't go there unless they are interested. And a lot of what you do with our social media profiles is useless unless you not only have awareness, but also interest. So, make sure to be interesting. ;)

LIKE

You have got them interested, and they are checking you out. If we use a fishing metaphor, they are nibbling on the bait, but you haven't hooked them yet. Now you need people to like you. People buy from those they like; it's as simple as that. Have you ever decided to buy something, walked into a shop, but then decided not to buy it there because something didn't feel right? Perhaps you didn't like the sales assistant or the shop itself. Maybe the parking lot annoyed you or the colour of their signage. Most of us have experienced this at one time or another. We might have even driven across town to buy whatever it was we wanted, and even paid a little more, just because we liked that store or the sales assistant better. Many people do business with certain businesses simply because they like them and think they are great. Apple, anyone? ;)

Just as with all human interaction and communication, everything is good in moderation, and it is important to be true to yourself and to your brand. If someone likes you and your brand, you are probably going to be good together. If you—or to be precise, your brand—try to be something you are not, people will see through it. Brands are like people, and nobody likes a fake. Authenticity is key.

At this stage of the process, don't try to sell anything. Just build up the relationship. Get permission from people to talk to them and tell them about interesting and useful things related to your product and service (note, *related to* your product or service – not *about* it). Give them value in some way. Why would they want to hang out with you? Let them get to know you, your brand, your business, your product or service, slowly and at their own pace. People don't like to be rushed. Make a deposit before you can make a withdrawal. Remember that date—don't pounce on them—give it time and get to know each other.

Remember to also be human. People do business with people, and people will buy from people they like. We don't really like to do business with companies per se. All things being equal, personality and the human connection wins.

Don't try to sell straight away—people don't like people who try to sell them stuff. Everyone likes to buy, but nobody likes to be sold to. Someone who helps them, on the other hand ... that's a different story. Remember, marketing is all about building relationships—don't ever forget that.

This is where a lot of your marketing activities come into play. Make sure people like what they see on your website and social media profiles. Nurture that relationship with them through your mailing list and all other interaction with them, whether it be in person, through email, telephone, or whatever. Content marketing, which we will discuss later in this book, is brilliant for this stage, and the next one, which is trust.

TRUST

The more people see you and interact with you, the more trust you build. Remember, we buy from those we trust. Trust is a fundamental thing in business. Without it, there is no business.

Repetition and frequency of contact are crucial in building trust. Think about it. Do you go to the same place regularly and see the same people but don't get to know them? Classic examples would be if you take classes with them, or go to the gym at the same time, or always do your weekly shop at the same time. You may be seeing the same face over and over again without knowing anything about the person or even saying hello.

Then you do a workshop or seminar and the instructor asks people to pair up. You don't know anyone there, but you see the woman who is always at the gym when you're there or the man who does his weekly shopping at the same time as you. You don't really know them at all, but chances are they are the first person you think to pair with? The reason is simple. You have seen them often and you trust them more than people you haven't seen before, no matter what else comes into play. It's human nature.

We always need trust. The larger the purchase decision, or the more personal the product or service, the more important trust becomes. Even if we are just buying a cheap piece of candy, we must trust that the company that sells it does their job properly, that the candy is not poisonous, old, stale, made with child labour, etc.

Trust is built through various ways. We already mentioned repetition and frequency. There is also consistency—don't change things up too much, or people won't know where they stand with you. It's the same in business as with personal relationships. We all know people we are uncomfortable around because we just don't quite know what to expect of them. One minute, they're lovely and fun; the next, they are cool and tough. It makes us uneasy and insecure, and we avoid being around them. The same is true with businesses. We want to know what to expect.

There is a multitude of other ways to build trust: Don't promise something you can't deliver. Have good and reliable information on your website. Use your LinkedIn company page and the profiles of you and your staff to show off your expertise, demonstrate what you have done in the past, your achievements, recommendations, endorsements, etc. This builds authority and credibility. If applicable, let people know that you, your staff, or your business have applicable qualifications, feature them on the website and at your office, shop, or other types of facilities. Customer testimonials build trust. Your brand identity builds trust, or tears it down, based on its presentation. Even if we don't consciously realise why, we are drawn to things that look clean and professional. Tatty signage, dirty floors, a letterhead obviously designed with Word Clipart, these things do not build trust. Have a good think about how you can build trust in your business and how you are doing this at the moment. Can you improve this?

TRIAL

It doesn't matter what we are buying, we always perceive any purchase as being a risk. The size of the risk depends on what you are buying – again, the more expensive or personal, the bigger the perceived risk. There is less risk in buying a lollipop than in buying a new car, but there is risk all the same. What if the lollipop tastes horrible? :)

This is why people prefer to try before they buy and, in some cases, will not buy unless they have a chance to test what they are purchasing.

If you have a product, this is fairly easy to deal with. People can go into a shop, check out the product, handle it, and even test it. If they buy online, they can return it. A car can be test driven; a house can be surveyed or inspected; you can have a return policy, a guarantee or warranty on your products to minimise risk to your customers.

When it comes to services, this is harder to do. It is the nature of service that you can't really know what it is like until you have used it, and once you have used it, you can't return it. You can't undo that haircut, return that massage, or unsleep in that hotel bed. Businesses can't decide not to buy those bookkeeping services once the accounts have been done, etc. So, you need to find ways for people to get a taste of what they will be getting. You need to find the best way possible for people to get an idea of what they will experience when using your service, to reduce the perceived risk to your potential buyers.

Ways to accomplish this include customer testimonials (they are like someone else trying things out for people), and videos that show the service in action can be a great way to build trust. Videos are also particularly powerful in giving people an idea of some sort of experience. Outlining processes can also be a great way to let people know what they will be buying ("this is how we work"). This can be done on your website or, if appropriate, explained in a meeting with the customer, with the help of visual aids. You can also give people a free trial period of a service, such as free for the first month, or for a considerably lower price. This is very well-known in the software business. A refund policy is another way of reducing risk (usually time limited).

Take some time to think about your business and how you can let people try your product or service before they buy.

SALE

Finally, we have arrived to what this is all about—the sale of your product or service. Once people get to this stage, you must make sure you have solid processes in place that move them as comfortably and easily as possible through the sales process.

There are a lot of things to think about here. How are you selling your product? If it is through a website, you need to make sure you have good and trustworthy payment services. How is the product delivered? Do you have instructions for the product's use once people buy it?

You have to be proactive and identify potential things that might go wrong. Classic examples include when you don't accept the customers' preferred method of payment. You may not accept their type of credit card or offer the financing they expect (can you match the competition?). Another classic example is the market stall that only accepts cash—the customer only has a card, and there is no cash machine anywhere nearby. The sale is lost.

The sales process varies greatly between different businesses, so I won't go into detail here. Just make sure you thoroughly review yours and make it as smooth as possible. Don't give your customers a reason not to go through with the purchase.

REPEAT SALES

Too many businesses seem to think the process ends with the sale. That's sooo not the case. This is where things really begin. It's the start of your marriage! You got that person to buy from you, so now you want them to buy again and again, as often as possible, and with as little time as possible between purchases. How are you going to do that?

There is a reason why things become clichés, and here is one for you: Depending on which source you quote, it costs between 5 to 16 times more to get a new customer than to hold on to an existing one. Whichever it is, it is a lot more expensive and a lot more work. It makes sense. Your customers are already aware of you and interested in you. After doing business with you, let's hope they still like you and trust you, and they have already tried your product or service. So, you want to keep the relationship with this customer going. You have already worked so hard to get her through the first 6 stages of the process; you can't just throw that away.

Of course, you also want to be getting new clients, but you definitely want to retain your existing ones. How can you best continue this relationship?

This varies between businesses, but there are tools that will help, such as customer email lists, online groups for customers only, offering any kind of additional value and help, and automated follow-up emails that are triggered at sale which send the buyer a message after a certain period of time. Entering customers into special loyalty programs can keep those customers with you and give you permission to stay in touch.

There has been research that shows that loyalty programs and such don't necessarily lead to growth; only getting new business can do that. This makes sense. However, there are three points I want to make: 1) You will want to hold your ground and keep the business you've got, and then you can keep adding to it. 2) Surely it is worth keeping that relationship going. You have already made contact with this person multiple times and built a relationship, so surely it is worth continuing it and trying to get more out of it, right? 3) Building a strong and longstanding relation-ship with your customers should increase the likelihood of them referring even more business to you, thereby creating new business.

Have systems in place to follow through once someone becomes a cus-tomer. For example, let's say the customer bought a camera from you. Soon after the purchase, you could send him an email to check how he is doing with it (an automatic email triggered by the sale, so you don't really have to do anything once it is set up) and tell him about a great lens that you have. Or send him a little booklet about photography and how to get the most out of his camera, including accessories that can enhance his experience even more, so he is even happier with his purchase—and happier with you, because you are so helpful and great.

If someone stayed at your hotel, you could have an automatic email sent later on thanking them for their stay, saying how much you loved to have them, and inviting them to please come again. Perhaps they came in the winter, so you could tell them how fantastic your area is in the summer: "You really must come again."

There are loads of simple little ways you can keep that relationship going, so take some time to think about what you could do in your business.

REFERRALS

The genius of all this is that, if you play your cards right, your customers can become a powerhouse of a marketing tool for you at little or no extra cost, by referring more business to you. However, we tend to just hope that they are happy with us and will tell people, rather than actively trying to influence this. As a result, we are leaving those referrals to chance.

You need specific tactics to encourage your customers to make referrals, giving you more business. The beauty of referrals is that they are a marketing tool that can lead a person through the marketing process to a sale in one fell swoop. Here's an example:

If my friend, Amy, asks me about a good hotel in Reykjavik, and I tell her about one:

1. Amy is going to be listening to me, as we are friends; therefore, she is aware of the hotel I mention just through that one point of contact (remember, people normally don't notice you straight away, it can take multiple points of contact just to get that awareness).

2. Amy will be interested when I tell her about the hotels I recommend—after all, she asked about it. And even if she hadn't

asked, and I was just telling her about it, she is likely to be interested in what I have to say (we are friends, after all ;)).

3. Amy likes me (she'd probably not be asking for my opinion if she didn't), so she figures that if I like something, she's likely to like it, too.

4. Amy trusts me (would you ask for advice from someone you don't trust?), so she trusts that I would only recommend something good—you could say that the trust rubs off me to the hotel I recommend.

5. Amy trusts me and that I have tried the hotel or that I at least know enough about it to know it's good; otherwise, I would not be referring it to her. In a way, I have gone through the trial part for her. Sure, she may want to check things out for herself, but she is going to be much more positive toward this hotel than if she just walked in off the street or stumbled upon it on the Internet.

6. Et voilà - we are at the sale!

You see, awareness, interest, like, trust, and trial by using just one marketing activity!

So, how can you encourage referrals? This can be done in many ways. Those emails you send to follow up on the sale and get repeat sales are perfect for also asking people to refer business or give you a recommendation. Reviews on websites are by their very nature referrals, so if there is a relevant website for your industry, encourage your customers to write reviews. Then there are classics like "bring a friend" or sign a friend up for something and the referrer gets a freebie. Customer testimonials are also a type of referral. There are loads of ways to do this. Think about what you could do to encourage referrals in your business – just don't leave it to chance! :)

How are you doing with the marketing process? Everything making sense?

Now, list all your marketing activities at the moment, and see if they cover all parts of the marketing process. And every time you do a marketing activity, keep the process in mind and what purpose within the marketing process that activity serves. That will help you ensure it is as effective as possible at getting people to the next stage.

Want ideas about things you can do to help each stage of your marketing process? Come join the *Marketing Untangled* community on Facebook and ask: facebook.com/groups/MarketingUntangledSeries. Not only will I reply, but you may get some great ideas from the community, as well! :)

Task: List each and every marketing activity you are using today and check whether you are covering all parts of the marketing process. What is the purpose of each of those marketing activities?

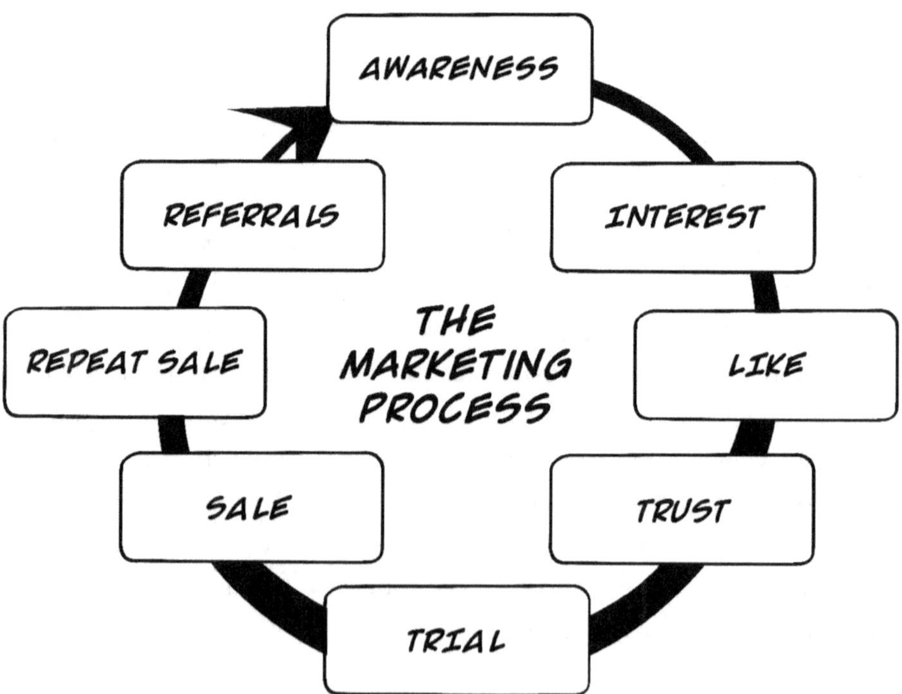

3. Lead Management

"...the aim of marketing is to make selling superfluous. The aim of marketing is to know and understand the customer so well that the product or service fits him and sells itself. Ideally, marketing should result in a customer who is ready to buy. All that should be needed then is to make the product or service available."[9]

— Peter Drucker

We have gone through the marketing process. That is the process your potential customer and customers go through, seen from *their* point of view. You may also have heard talk about customer or buyer journeys, AIDA, funnels or some other way to represent it. The important thing is to realise how it works and that you need to steer people through this process, or lead them, and to do that, you need to make sure you have the right tools and methods. In marketing jargon, this is often called "lead management". A "lead" is a person who comes into the marketing process because they are aware of you and interested. They are a potential customer.

It is important to know exactly how you are managing your leads. Which marketing activities are you using? Why? What do you want them to do? How do you make sure they all work together to lead people through the process? It is also important to realise that few, if any, marketing activities can sell on their own. If it seems like they do, think again. Is it really that simple, or could it be that you were lucky in that the person was looking for exactly what you had to offer at that time and that place? Has that person perhaps been checking the market for a long time and is finally ready to buy? There can be lots of reasons for them buying at that moment, and it would be naive to think that just one action on your part is that powerful. You must realise that you need to do a lot of things to get people to buy ... and remember not to get despondent. Even if they don't buy now, keep at it, and they could buy later. I've had people attend my talks and then come to me three years later, when they are ready to do the work!

A story that illustrates the marketing process in action is when I bought three copies of a children's book that greeted me at the entrance of the supermarket one day. It would be an easy mistake to think that just having the books displayed in a flashy promotional stand at the entrance did the trick. When I thought about it, I realised that I had been aware of the author for years. He had appeared in children's plays and movies in Iceland and is also very well known to adults through his music and radio appearances. Awareness—check! The book was about science for children, which piqued my interest. I'd seen a lot of the author throughout the years, liked what I'd seen, experienced his other work, and was in need of presents for a few children – spot on. Because of his previous work, I knew I could trust this was something good. The fact that it was promoted and sold in this particular supermarket also helped. On the stand, they had a book with no seal, that I could quickly leaf through to see the contents—a trial. And there I was, at the checkout, buying three copies to give as presents. It only took a couple of minutes to make the purchase decision, but only because the groundwork had been laid over a much longer time—years even.

Research, particularly in B2B markets, has shown that people are between 50-70 percent of their way through the marketing process before even contacting the business in question.[10] It seems probable that this also applies in B2C markets and may even be higher. People gather information through various methods: online, through media, friends and family, etc. before coming to you. Therefore, you need to make sure you are where they are, giving them the information they need when they need it so they will eventually come. Of course, with online sales, they may never really "come to you"; they may buy without ever talking to a member of staff or coming to your location at all.

Managing your "leads" this way also saves you a lot of work. When people finally contact your business, they have already done a lot of research and information gathering and are much closer to buying, which means that your staff needs a lot less time with them, making things more efficient. It can also mean that those who are not likely to buy have dropped out in the earlier stages already, so you are not wasting your time on them. This is pure marketing, because, as Drucker says in the quote at the beginning of this chapter, when marketing is done properly, you don't need sales techniques or tactics; you just need someone to service the customer, perhaps answer a few questions, and then ring up the cash register.

To clarify, I think it is important to mention that if you were to search for "lead management" on Google, you will get a lot of information about very sophisticated marketing software solutions designed to help you lead people through the process. These software solutions are outside the scope of this book and will, therefore, not be discussed here. They vary greatly in price and complexity and are often designed with specific industries and types of businesses in mind. We are going to look at the process itself and how you can bring people through it with general tools, rather than complex and expensive marketing automation software. If you want to explore the software side further, I suggest you search for "lead management software" or "marketing automation software" online and do your research well before making the large investment in money, work, and time that they require.

We can present the lead management process next to the marketing process as shown in the picture below. Take a moment to look at the illustration, and then we will look at each stage in turn.

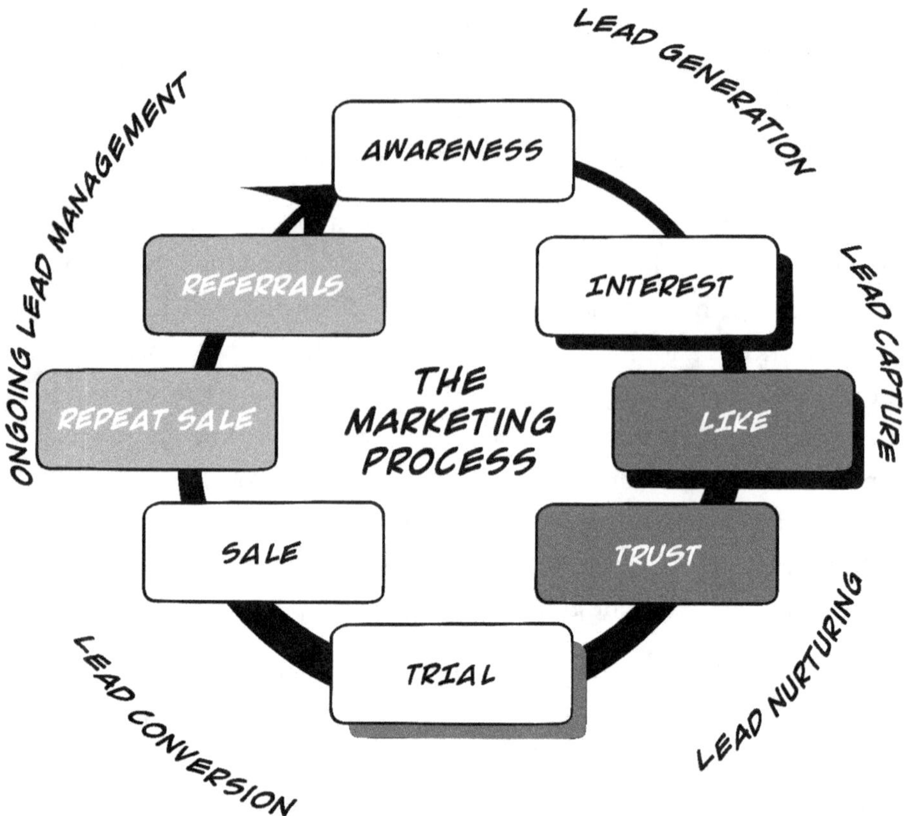

Lead Generation

Lead generation refers to generating awareness and interest—reaching people. You want to let people know you exist and get them interested in order to start moving them through the marketing process. You are "generating," or producing, leads, or possible customers who know about you and are interested in finding out more. Advertising is a classic example of a marketing activity that is useful for lead generation.

Generally, you can say that with lead generation, you can either work for things or pay for them. You can do a lot of things without directly spending money; for example, you can use various tactics to more easily get found online, guest post for high-traffic blogs, and use social media to get traffic to a web page where you can continue the process, or you can simply pay for exposure through online advertising and advertising through social media to get that web traffic. It is your choice. The free activities will require more work, so if you have some money to spend, you might want to take a shortcut and pay, even if it is just to get the ball rolling.

Search engine optimisation (SEO)—activities that aim at getting your webpage or other online content to the top of the search results on Google, Bing, Yahoo, and other search engines—and content marketing are both examples of things that, if used well, can generate leads. Content marketing is actually at the heart of SEO and is all about delivering content in various forms that your target audience finds interesting and will, therefore, link to online, share on social media, etc. This then builds your brand and your relationship with them to aid sales. Good content that gets shared is important in the way search engines evaluate the most relevant search results to show. The content needs to be interesting and of good quality, and it should have value to people, whilst also creating awareness of you, your business, products, and services. Recency also plays a big role, so this is something that you continually need to work at. Social media is also a good lead generator and very much ties in with SEO and content marketing.

Offline lead generation activities can include traditional media advertising, taking part in exhibitions, public speaking, and various other methods.

Lead Capture

As the phrase indicates, lead capture activities capture those leads that have been generated by lead generation activities. Your goal is to continue staying in touch with people and build your relationship with them with less effort and money than in the lead generation stage. As you will have realised when looking at the marketing process, it takes quite a lot of contact with your business, product, or service before people are prepared to buy. If you have to pay each time you want to talk to them to build that relationship—for example, by using advertising or spending a lot of effort by getting exposure through social media and other means—it can quickly get expensive. If you were running a huge business with marketing budgets like Coca Cola, Unilever, or Procter & Gamble, then, yes, you can pay for maintaining that relationship through traditional media advertising and such ways, but as small and medium businesses or entrepreneurs, few, if any, of us can afford to rely on those methods.

You want to capture people by hooking them in in some way. The most common, popular, and as indicated by research and experience to be the most powerful, method is building a list of email subscribers that are happy to receive regular emails from you. To some extent, getting followers on social media can do this, but with those, you are always relying on a medium not controlled by you to deliver the message, and there are no guarantees of visibility. Free and organic visibility on social media has been dwindling fast, particularly when it comes to the giant of social media networks, Facebook. Capturing the leads into a platform that you control and that doesn't require you to pay each time you want to contact people has often been likened to owning, rather than renting, your marketing. If they are on your email list, you can email them without having to pay through the nose each time; but if you rely on advertising, you have to pay each time—and often you have to pay whether you reach the specific people you want or not.

The goal is to get people's permission to stay in touch. Only by giving them something they want, something they are interested in and value, can you do that. Just as they can sign up to stay in touch, they can unsubscribe—or, in the case of social media, they can unfollow, unlike, etc. Content marketing—where you are giving them content that they really want—is, therefore, again crucial in this phase of the lead management process, because if you are giving them what they want, they are more likely to stick around (incidentally, you need to know your target group very well to know what they want ;)).

Lead Nurturing

Lead nurturing is all about nurturing this relationship you have established with your potential customers. Content marketing through email is again a strong tool here. Through your content, you can get people to like you and you can build trust.

This stage of the process takes time. As you know, people are not ready to buy from you straight away—no more than someone is ready to marry you after the first date. It will depend on your market, your product, service, and various other things how long this can take. Theoretically, things can happen very fast, even within a day or a week, but in many industries (particularly in B2B markets), this process can take months or even years. It is always better to assume that it will take a while to nurture the relationship before people are ready to buy—if it takes a shorter amount of time, that's a great bonus! But by giving it time, this could lead to a longer and more loyal relationship.

Think about what people want to know before they are prepared to buy from you. Tell them about those things. Show them that you are the right business for them. Think carefully about the marketing process. What can you do to get people to like you and trust you, and how can you give them a chance to sample your product or "get a taste" of your service? Don't just start selling right away. Build that relationship and then gradually introduce your products and services.

It is an interesting human trait that if we have started a relationship, in however small a way (such as signing up for an email list), we are more likely to be prepared to take gradually larger steps in that relationship. It's a bit like romance. The other person is unlikely to walk down the aisle straight away. Start by inviting them out for coffee, segue to dinner, and after a few dates, things may start happening. Play your cards right, and you may be booking a wedding venue before you know it!

If someone is prepared to subscribe to your emails (a small payment of an email address), the next thing they may be prepared to do is share your content with others, thereby validating you by putting their name to yours. The next step may be to buy something small and inexpensive from you, then something bigger, and so on and so forth, until you have a loyal and lucrative customer.

If you look at the most skilled internet marketers, this process can be seen very, very clearly:

1. Sign up to an email list in exchange for something free—no money, simple to do.

2. Sign up for a free webinar—no money, fairly straightforward, but you are committing time to attend the webinar.

3. An affordable product, whether a course, eBook, or other offering. Priced in a way that it is not a big decision, not something you have to think about for long. Often between the $7 to $20 mark, depending on the market.

4. Then they offer you a bigger product, but still not so big that it needs great consideration. Let's say somewhere between $50 and $200.

5. Only then do they offer you their big program, and perhaps a VIP package or something like that. It costs more, but you also get more. Here we may be talking somewhere between $500-$2,000.

6. You may even be offered one more than that, a seminar or a retreat, for example, for a considerable amount of money, as well as the commitment of time and the cost and hassle of travel. But

they won't try to offer that to you right off the bat. They only do that once they have spent quite a bit of time and effort building their relationship with you and may even only offer this to people who have purchased something from them before.

These skilled and experienced marketers would never dive straight in and try to sell you a weekend package at $3,000 plus travel and accommodation, because they know you are not ready. The relationship hasn't been nurtured, and the trust and like factors have not been built.

This can sound like people are being tricked, but if you think about it, that's really not what it is about. It is a question of giving people what they want. Those who are interested will buy the less expensive products and services; those who are even more interested will buy the next one up, etc. The marketer also only spends their time and effort on the people likeliest to buy by qualifying the lead at each stage of the process.

The exact execution of this phase of the process will depend very much on your market and industry, so you need to examine this carefully for yourself.

Lead Conversion

Lead conversion is all about sealing the deal, converting the leads to paying customers.

Up until now, you have been nurturing the relationship, letting people get to know you and getting to know them. Now you need activities to get them to take that step of buying. You need to give them an opportunity to try your product or service in some way, thereby reducing their perceived risk in buying (trial). People always perceive some risk in buying, so you must be aware of that and make sure you have tools and activities in place to counteract that perception. You also need to give people a little nudge to get them to act now, to make the decision to buy, pull out their wallet and do it today, not tomorrow or next year.

Man is a creature of procrastination. Inertia is ingrained in our DNA. Most people simply don't act. They simply don't do. People may be aware of your product or service, interested in it, like it, trust it, and they might have even tried it and loved it, but they still may not buy. So, they need a little nudge.

If you have ever seen anything I do, or even if you have just been reading this book, you will know that I am all about marketing; I do not stand for sales techniques or trickery. I firmly believe the Drucker quote mentioned earlier that basically says that if marketing does its job, *"all that should be needed is to make the product or service available."*

That being said, here are a few things that can help nudge the lead toward being converted to a customer. Use them carefully and honestly—I cannot stress that enough. These are not tricks. They are not designed to deceive or be used in any dishonest way, although they can be used that way, as can so many other things that are not made for bad purposes. They can, however, help make people decide and make them act and action is crucial.

For more on this, I recommend reading *Influence* by Robert Cialdini—a marketing classic.

Social Proof

We are social beings that have a tendency to follow the herd and do as others do. It's simply human nature. If people see that others approve of your product or service, they are much more likely to approve it themselves. Remember the story of the emperor's new clothes? That would be the negative side to social proof and herd behaviour.

So, what kind of activities can you use to provide social proof? Here are some examples:

- Customer testimonials
- Highlighting media coverage about you, your business, product, or service, as appropriate
- Telling people how many others have bought—remember those "join 2,000 happy customers" phrases?

With all of the above, people tend to think that if someone else thinks this is great, it must be great. Knowing that others have bought and are happy simply makes people feel better about making that choice. "All these people can't be wrong, can they?"

Fear of Losing Out

This is also called loss aversion (and FOMO or fear of missing out ;)). No one wants to miss out. If you feel like a good opportunity might be slipping through your fingers, this can often be enough to get you to take that step of buying. Quite a few sources find that people are more scared of losing something than they are happy about gaining something.[11] Therefore, it can be much more effective to talk about how much people might lose by not buying than about how much they will gain by buying.

Communicate what people might lose out on if they don't buy from you ... but be aware of not becoming too negative—too much negativity can also push people away. So, talk about potential gains, as well—pepper them in, if you will.

We all recognise phrases like the ones below, but they are used because they work to get people to make a decision, take action, and buy. This won't make anyone buy who doesn't really want to; it will just give those who do a little push. What phrases? Well, phrases like these:

- "Don't miss this opportunity..."
- "Are you missing out..."
- "Stop wasting your time and ..."

Another way of doing this is the scarcity play. Indicate that something is only available for a limited time or in a limited quantity and, therefore, you need to act now in order not to miss out:

- "Only ... left!"
- "While stocks last"
- "Must end May 15th"

Putting a timeframe on your offer is often enough to get people to act and buy. Just remember, people will see through a lie, so if there isn't really a time limit or limited quantity, don't say there is.

Throwing an Anchor

The concept of anchoring is well known from negotiation techniques. The first number mentioned will always become the benchmark to which everything else will be held. We live in an extremely complicated world, so we constantly compare things to help us make decisions. Is this better than that? Should I do this or that? The first price we see will always be the price all other prices for comparable things are compared against. "Hey, these jeans are much cheaper than the ones at the other shop!" "Wow, this book is much more expensive than the one online."

This is the reason why you won't just see the sale price, but also the original price. The original price becomes the anchor and the frame of reference for calculating how much you gain by buying on sale. If you see something that used to be $49.99 and is now $25.99, you perceive that as a much better deal than something that was and is simply $25.99.

Another way to use this is to use the "now" call to action. "Buy **now** at this price." You cannot avoid thinking that now is, therefore, better than before or better than it will be. You can also do this by using bonuses—not necessarily changing the actual price but stating that right now you will get more for your money. The book you published last year is *now available with a free workbook*, or the shampoo you always buy is now 3-for-2, etc. People will compare: "I didn't get this before, and it may not be available later, so I gain by buying this now."

Remove the Risk!

Whatever we are buying, we perceive risk. Find ways to reduce that risk through things like social proof, but also by giving good information about the product or service, giving people the option of returning the product, cancelling the service, and offering guarantees, warranties, and such.

Shiny New Things!

We are suckers for novelty. The new iPhone, the newest model of that car, this season's collection. If you have a reason to say there is something new, do so. Who hasn't heard of "new and improved?" It's used a lot because it works! Have you seen those queues outside the Apple stores when they release a new iPhone or gadget?! "New" just might be the thing that makes people take action and buy from you.

Ongoing Lead Management

Ongoing lead management is all about continuing the relationship with your customer and, therefore, increasing the likelihood of them buying from you again and referring your business. This works much the same as lead nurturing, except you need to keep in mind that you are now further building a relationship with people who have already bought from you, so the content and information you provide need to take that into account.

You can do things like having further information and guidance for your products and services on your website, or a special email list for customers who receive "inside information" and even better deals or the ability to buy new things before they are released to the general public. Offer them something to make them feel special, like VIPs. You can also use online groups to do this kind of thing. Build a community where you stay in touch and become a part of their lives. Also, think about how you can possibly encourage referrals (more on that later).

A lot of the concepts discussed in this section will be discussed in more detail in the individual marketing activities that are covered later in this book. What is important to take and remember from this section is how people need to be moved through the marketing process, that you need to have the activities in place to do that, and consciously use everything you do with a clear purpose. Also, remember that things do not happen by themselves. Referrals are a good example of something that we tend to just hope for, instead of actively asking for them. If you don't ask, you won't get. ;)

Take a look at the reader resources at thoranna.is/mcureader for further examples of marketing activities suitable for each phase of the lead management process.

Patience is a Virtue

It is very important to remember that marketing takes time. You must constantly be repeating the same message. Your brand needs to be constantly hammered in, everywhere you possibly can and as often as you possibly can. Your customer needs to get to know you before they are ready to buy. How long it takes depends on a number of things, such as what your product or service is, the price point, your market environment, and more. According to sales guru Brian Tracy, a salesman needs five sales visits before the prospect is ready to buy. This means you will stand face to face with and talk to the customer on five occasions (which, by the way, is a very expensive way of selling, and I don't recommend you do it, with very, very few exceptions). Hence, you can expect that you need a lot more contact through other types of marketing communications before people are prepared to buy.

There is a fantastic quote from Thomas Smith, from the year 1885, on how often a man needs to see an ad before he buys:[12]

- The first time a man looks at an advertisement, he does not see it.
- The second time, he does not notice it.
- The third time, he is conscious of its existence.
- The fourth time, he faintly remembers having seen it before.
- The fifth time, he reads it.
- The sixth time, he turns up his nose at it.
- The seventh time, he reads it through and says, "Oh brother!"
- The eight time, he says "Here's that confounded thing again!"
- The ninth time, he wonders if it amounts to anything.
- The tenth time, he asks his neighbour if he has tried it.
- The eleventh time, he wonders how the advertiser makes it pay.
- The twelfth time, he thinks it must be a good thing.
- The thirteenth time, he thinks perhaps it might be worth something.
- The fourteenth time, he remembers wanting such thing for a long time.
- The fifteenth time, he is tantalized because he cannot afford to buy it.

- The sixteenth time, he thinks he will buy it someday.
- The seventeenth time, he makes a memorandum to buy it.
- The eighteenth time, he swears at his poverty.
- The nineteenth time, he counts his money carefully.
- The twentieth time he sees the ad, he buys what it is offering.

That was in 1885. Can you imagine what it's like now with the amount of marketing messages we are bombarded with every day!

Patience is, therefore, a virtue in marketing, and you need to constantly repeat the same message over and over and over again from every possible direction.

4. Lead Them

I hope it is clear from the discussion about the marketing process and the lead management system that people need to be led through the process, toward the sale and beyond. Therefore, you need to carefully consider how you connect all your marketing activities to move people through.

No matter what you are doing in your marketing, always think about what you want that particular marketing activity to do and what you want people to do next. If you advertise, what do you want that advert to do? It can only do one thing—believe me, advertising cannot accomplish many things at once. It is accomplishment enough if it does the one thing you want it to do; do not expect it to do more! As a result of the ad, do you want people to sign up to your email list? Facebook ads have proven to be great for that, if used correctly, by giving people something for free when they sign up to the mailing list. Big corporations may have enough money to advertise just to get visibility and awareness and stay at the top of our minds, but those of us running smaller businesses just can't afford that. You need your marketing activities, advertising and all, to work just as hard as you do for your business, preferably harder!

Then what? Let's say you've advertised something for free when people sign up, and they have subscribed. The next step would be to nurture that lead. When you have done that, you want to convert them into customers, etc.

How are you going to get people to do what you want them to do? Well, what's the most obvious way? Simply to ask. And you know what—it is also the most effective. ;) In marketing jargon, we call this "Call to Action," often shortened to CTA. We all know them; they're phrases such as "Subscribe," "Sign Up," "Buy Now," "Click Here" etc. Those clear and concise words tell you exactly what to do.

As with most things in marketing, there are a lot of theories behind how to craft the perfect call to action, particularly when it comes to online marketing. All sorts of things have been tested: where should it be placed, what colours work best, what words, how large should it be, etc. I won't go into detail here—it could be the subject of another book entirely, and also, there is a lot of debate about what works and what doesn't. The best way to find out is simply to test it and see what works. There are, however, three things that you must always keep in mind when it comes to your Calls to Action:

1. Clearly tell people what you want them to do: "click here," "come into the store," "visit our website for more information," "buy," "sign-up," "forward to a friend," etc.

2. Tell them how to do it—make it crystal clear. "Click *this* button" or "click *this* link," "go to this website," "go to this place and do that," "do this and then this will happen," etc. There should be no doubt about how to do it and what the process is like—and no surprises.

3. The biggest one: Tell them why! Why should they do it? What's in it for them? What do they get if they do what you are asking them to do?

In his book, *The New Rules of Marketing and PR*, David Meerman Scott says, "Nobody cares about your products or services except you."[13] He could not be more right! People don't care. They only care about what they get out of things and what things do for them. So, if you want them to do something, you need to make it very clear why it is good for them to do exactly that. Will it help them lose 10kg in a month? Will it increase sales by ten percent in the next six weeks? Will it make them happier, prettier, smarter? What will people get from what it is you want them to do? And this does not just apply at the very end. It's not just why they should fork out the money and buy your stuff, but earlier in the marketing process, as well. Why should they like your page on Facebook? Why should they sign up for your email list? Why should they attend that meeting? Always remember that people will ask themselves, "What's in it for me?" and if there isn't enough in it, they won't do what you are asking them to do.

5. Measure

How is your marketing going? Good? Great! How do you know?

There is a reason for that old saying: "You can't manage what you can't measure." You need to measure your results. Otherwise, you have no way of knowing whether what you are doing is working. You must be clear on what you want your marketing activities to do and how you are going to know whether they are doing it or not. The small business owners and entrepreneurs I know, including myself, don't have the time or resources to be doing things that don't work. I'm sure you don't, either. The only way to make sure you are not wasting your efforts is to measure your results.

There is no way for me to create an exhaustive list of ways to measure the results of your marketing efforts. It all depends on what you are doing, how your activities interact, and what you want them to do. If you advertise in the local paper, offering people a free demonstration on Thursday night, you want to make sure you count how many people show up on that night. And remember – if you advertised through other ways, you also have to consider how you can know who came based on the ad in the paper and who came because of something else. If you ask people to book an appointment to get a free interview, you want to measure how many people do. If you want more traffic to your website or ecommerce site, you can use Google Analytics to track your traffic and see where most of it is coming from and, hence, what is working the best, and where it is *not* coming from, so you can fix that or drop it.

If you have an online store, you want to know how many of you visitors actually buy. If a lot of people visit the website but no one is buying, you know you don't have a traffic problem; you have a conversion problem and need to work on your site to fix that.

For each and every activity you use and for your marketing program as a whole, you need to examine things like that: What do you want it to do? Is it doing it? Why? Why not? You can't afford to waste time and effort on things that don't work. You need to know whether things are working, and you want to know as soon as possible. If they are not, you want to fix them, and if you find they can't be fixed and simply don't work for you, you want to drop them so that you can focus your efforts and resources on things that do work. And if you find out that what you are doing is working great, that's fantastic! Do more of it! Get even more out of your efforts!

That's it for Part I of this book. Hopefully, it has given you a better understanding of the things to consider when choosing your marcoms activities. If you have any questions, please do join the *Marketing Untangled* Facebook community at facebook.com/groups/MarketingUntangled-Series. But now, let's have a look at the myriad of ingredients you have to play with when creating your marketing program!

PART II

Marketing Activities

This section of the book contains a huge list of marketing activities. They have been divided into five categories and listed in alphabetical order within those categories (not in order of importance or effectiveness!):

Priority 1: Marketing Activities You Must Use

These are the kinds of things you must have in place, no matter what business or industry you are in, and these need to be done as soon as possible. Some of them take little time and effort, such as setting up an email signature, but others are bigger projects, such as building a website or doing search engine optimisation. If you have been in business for a while, you may already have a lot of these things in place.

Priority 2: Marketing Activities You Must Use but Not Until After Priority 1!

These are things we all need to use, but they are not as urgent as those in Priority 1. Therefore, don't start putting these in place until you have covered the Priority 1 activities, or they are at least well underway.

Priority 3: Marketing Activities You May Want to Use

In Priority 3, you will find activities that most businesses may want to use. This includes a lot of useful things, and I encourage you to examine them well and choose the ones you find suitable for you. Some of them may actually be Priority 2 for you, but they will not be that for everyone.

A Few Ideas to Keep Handy

This one is a collection of lots of ideas. By all means, run through them and see if there are any you think could be useful for you or that you may want to keep in mind for a later date. Do not think you need to use all of them, and by all means, don't use them until you have covered Priorities 1, 2, and 3 and have the activities you are using from those under your belt.

Social Media

I have separated social media from the rest, as it is such a large subject. I have yet to find a business that cannot benefit from being on at least some of them, so they really belong in Priority 1. But even if they have their separate section, I will only cover the main ones. There is such a multitude of them that there is no way all of them can be covered, and things develop so fast that the book would be out-of-date before it came to print if I went into too much detail. You will find more resources in the reader resources for the book at thoranna.is/mcureader because it is simply much easier for me to add to and amend the information online.

A few important things to keep in mind when going through this section:

Going through this can feel a bit overwhelming. It is important to remember that you don't need to do all of it—I am simply giving you quite a comprehensive (but by no means exhaustive) list of options from which to choose. Choose the options that are right for you—you can think of it like choosing from a menu. :) As discussed in chapter 3, you need to choose your marketing activities based on where your target groups are, what your brand is, how you build your lead management system to guide people through the marketing process, and last, but not least, what is right for you.

Start with the Priority 1 activities, then Priority 2, and only then move on to the ones you want to use from Priority 3. The ideas are just that: Ideas. They are something to check out and use when you feel ready.

This can, of course, never be an exhaustive list of all the marketing activities out there. That is impossible. Nor can it go into each of them in any real depth. Many of them warrant books of their own. However, I hope it will give you ideas and point you in the right direction. I have also gathered more information and links to useful resources in the reader resources at thoranna.is/mcureader.

It's All About the Money

You will notice when you go through the list that I have not included traditional big budget media advertising. This is a book for small- and medium-sized businesses and entrepreneurs. Few, if any, of us can afford to use big budget marketing activities effectively. They simply cost too much, and their results are extremely hard to measure. I am not saying that you should not use them, but I advise you to start with the kinds of activities discussed in this book and then see if you need to go down the big budget media route—and whether you can afford to. It's easy to spend a lot of money on old style traditional marketing, and you can get good sales from it, but it tends not to leave a lot of money in the till. Surely, that's not the point. You want effective marketing that doesn't cost the earth and leaves profits for you, right? So, you won't find anything here about TV ads, radio ads, or print ads, but you will find a heck of a lot of other things. So, let's go for it!

Priority 1: Marketing Activities You Must Use

Brand Identity and Tone of Voice

The look of everything you do, your brand identity, needs to reflect the brand character you want to build. You could say that your brand is like a person and the brand identity is the clothes she wears. The way your brand looks is important and can make or break whether people want to do business with you.

The look of your brand can have a major say in whether people notice your brand and in getting you **awareness**. It can also be **interesting** and **like**able. A professional look helps build **trust,** and a consistent look helps people remember you, thereby helping you not only get the **sale** but also the **repeat sale**–and keeping you top of mind so that when asked, people **refer** business to you.

The tone of your brand refers to how it speaks, whether in the spoken or written word. The choice of words and the way they are put forward can help you get interest, but if you are not careful, they may have a negative effect on people. Think about the people you know and how the way they speak influences your views of them. In the same way, the way your brand speaks is important. The right tone can get attention, interest, be likeable, and build trust.

Brand identity and tone of voice is discussed in more detail in *Branding Untangled*, the previous book in the *Marketing Untangled* Series, so if this is something you want to get more out of, I recommend you grab a copy and get reading.

Business Card

Business Cards for Individuals

Professional and good-looking business cards with clear information may travel far and wide. If you are working internationally, consider having them in English, as well as your own language. Your business card should include the following information:

- Name and job title
- Business logo
- Business name
- Business address, if relevant
- Your email
- Main telephone number
- Your mobile number
- Your website domain
- Your social media URLs
- One line that explains what you or your business does (tagline)

Don't forget, your business card can pack a punch. People often save them or scan them into their contact database. Think whether you can put anything more on your business card that might make it work even harder for you. Make sure, though, that it does not get too cluttered—listen to your designer when she says enough is enough. ;) Your business card may be the first thing people see of you, for example, if they are given one with a referral.

Within the marketing process, business cards can be useful in many ways.

- Don't be stingy when it comes to your business cards. Give them to whoever will take them. You never know where they end up and the **awareness** they may create.

- When used in referrals and when interesting, business cards can pique people's **interest** and, more often than not, lead to people checking out your website or your social media profiles, leading them on their merry way down the marketing process.

- By having your information handy, your customers always know where to find you for that **repeat purchase**.

- Be generous with giving a few business cards to your customers and business network in general and encourage them to give them to those that may be interested. This is a great way to encourage **referrals**.

Business Cards for Your Business

A business card for your business is exactly that—a general card for your business, rather than individuals within it. They can be used in various ways, such as by making them visible and accessible in relevant places (for example, a financial consultant and a marketing consultant could feature each other's business cards, or a hairdresser and a beautician could feature each other).

These cards can be a good tool to help others refer business to you when business cards for individual employees may not be appropriate.

General business cards can be useful in getting awareness and interest. This type of business card should at least have the following information:

- Business name
- Business logo
- Business address, if relevant
- General email, i.e., business@business.com or info@business.com

- Main telephone number
- Website address
- Social media URLs
- A line that describes what your business does (tagline)

As with business cards for individuals within the business, these business cards can help at different stages in the marketing process (see above).

All business cards, whether general or for individuals, should of course have the same appearance as every other brand identity asset.

Domain Name

Your domain name, or URL, is important. It needs to be easy to remember and preferably it's simply the name of your business, product, or service. If you can't get your business name as a domain name, you can add something simple to the name, but it needs to make sense, for example, explain what you do. Social media scheduling tool Buffer had the domain bufferapp.com for a long time before being able to afford to buy buffer.com, and early Dropbox adopters will remember when their URL was getdropbox.com. Your domain name is closely linked to your name, and you need to consider this when choosing a name for your business, product, or service.

You also need to think about which domain ending you will use – those little letters at the end. What suits will depend on your business, but the major one is .com and national endings such as .co.uk or .is (for Iceland ;) .) There are lots more available now—there is even a .marketing domain ending! Hmmm, thoranna.marketing - what do you think? ;)

You may want more than one domain. If you operate in an international market, you may want to own your country domain, as well as .com and country domains in any other countries you operate in. Think about the future. Where are you heading with your business? Will you be going global? You may want to secure those domain names straight away. Even if you don't set up separate websites for each country or language, you can always have the domain redirect to your main one; for example, if people were to put in *nameofbusiness.co.uk*, they would end up at *nameofbusiness*.com.

Note that you can buy (or, actually, rent) your domain straight away even though you may not use it until later. You can check for and buy domain names in many places. A couple that I have good experience with using in the past are Europeregistry.com and GoDaddy.com.

Your domain name won't help increase awareness or interest, because people need to know about it to use it. However, if people are interested in finding out more about you, the first thing they might do is type what they think your domain name will be into their browsers, often starting with your brand name and .com, so having that .com is a good thing. However, don't fret if you are not able to get a straightforward domain name like that. In today's world, if people want to find you, they will do an online search for you, so as long as you have a domain that is closely related to your business name, and do basic search engine optimisation for that name, they should find you. More on SEO later. ;)

A good domain name can help with the **trust** factor for your business. It makes it a "proper" business, having a professional domain with a recognised domain ending.

Email at Your Own Domain

A real business has its own email address. That is just the way it is. If your business has @hotmail.com, @gmail.com, @yahoo.com, or similar email account, you are giving out a signal that you are not a proper business. Why would you do that?

Make sure you have an email address on your own domain. You will need a domain for your website anyway, and email services often come with web hosting. The costs should not be an issue and are definitely not prohibitive when it comes to getting an email address on your own domain.

Personally, I am a huge fan of G Suite from Google and run all my businesses on that, with various different domains. It is a cost effective and convenient solution that offers so much more than just email, like Google Drive online storage, Google Docs, Calendar, and Sites.

An email on your own domain is important when it comes to building *trust* in your business. Real businesses have emails on their own domains; that's just the way it is. Why let a little thing like a generic email address indicate that you may not be serious about what you do? ;)

Email Signature

Your email signature is part of your marketing materials and probably one of the most widely travelled—and it's completely free! Your email signature can help your marketing by displaying your company logo, your name and contact information, and any additional messages you may want to communicate.

Are you sure your email signature is doing everything it can for you? ;)

Your email signature should include the following:

- Greeting
- Name and position
- Logo
- Name of company
- Address, if your physical location is relevant to your customers
- Email

- Telephone number and mobile number, if appropriate
- Your website URL as a link
- Social media URLs as links with a call to action to join you there (like us, follow us, connect, etc.)
- One line about what your business does (tagline)

How your email signature is set up on your computer will affect the way your recipients see it. If you use an image, the signature may show up as an attachment to the email, which not only can be annoying, but it also means that the recipient does not see the image. On the other hand, an image can be quite effective and could even be a small ad that travels widely through your emails. Make sure, however, that any basic information is not in an image but written in the signature, so it always appears. This applies to URLs, also. Only your logo and an ad, if you want, should be as images.

Make sure that the look of your signature and the font and colours are the same as in any of your other brand visual elements. All your staff's email signatures should look the same.

If your brand font is not a system font, and, therefore, not generally available on all computers (Mac or PC), you should select a system font that closely resembles your brand font. This way you can make sure it appears the same on all computers. Otherwise, things may go very wrong somewhere and look awful—and you won't even know about it! ;)

We all sometimes send emails to people who have never heard from us before or our emails may be forwarded (I must stress that all unsolicited marketing emails are illegal in most countries, certainly in the EU, US, UK, and Iceland). Why not make a proper mark with a proper signature and thereby create *awareness*? It might even arouse their *interest* and get them to check you out some more. An interesting brand tone of voice in your signature, interesting information, and such can also be *like*able and have a positive impact. :)

A professional email signature with all the necessary information can build **trust** and sends a signal that you are a proper and credible business. Your signature can also increase the effect of your continued contact with people by letting them know about new products and such, helping you get more *sales*.

Keyword Analysis

How we shop has changed drastically, even if we only look to the turn of the century. People now go online to get information about products and services, turning to search engines and social media on their phones or computers. Google is at the top of the search engine heap, but we cannot ignore other search engines, such as Yahoo and Bing. Generally speaking, however, if you optimise for Google, you should be fine with the others. ;)

When looking for things, people write words and phrases into the search engine, and the engine then finds the most relevant websites and pages for those word and phrases. It is important to rank for the right words, thereby attracting the right people in the right mindset, to your website.

As with any everything else in your marketing, it is dangerous to assume things. You might think people will use certain words and phrases to search, but that's not necessarily so. You are an expert in your field. People who are not experts might use a vocabulary that is nothing like the words used within the industry and very often don't know the industry jargon. Also, sometimes people don't really know what it is they are looking for. Therefore, you need to do a keyword analysis to find out what people are actually using. Don't just assume you know.

You need to find the right keywords and phrases for you, your business, product, or service. Find the words and phrases people actually use to look for them. Luckily, in the Internet age, this information is quite easily available, so you don't have to guess. How complicated this process is depends on what kind of business you are in and your market. For some businesses you might easily be able to do this yourself with a bit of guidance; for others, getting an expert on board may be necessary. Whichever it is, it is always good to understand what is involved so you can better work with the experts you hire. It is always good to be an informed buyer. ;)

It is not just for your website that you need to analyse keywords and optimise for search. If you know the right keywords to use, you can also increase your chances of getting found elsewhere online and bring people in from there. Using your keywords on social media profiles, in news releases, and more, can help lead the right people, in the right frame of mind, to your website or your door.

Good keyword analysis is also a crucial part of online advertising, such as pay-per-click ads (Google Ads probably being the best-known platform for those), whether they appear on search engine results pages or on various other places on the web.

Keyword analysis is clearly a tool for the **awareness** phase of the marketing process. When people search for things like those that you have to offer, keyword analysis and the right use of those keywords can make all the difference in getting found. It can also be argued that effective keyword analysis and usage is a factor in building **trust**, because if you are at or toward the top of the search results, people will believe that you are good at what you do. Google lends trust. ;)

Local Listings

Make sure you are listed in any relevant local directory listings. This will be different between countries, so you need to do a little digging to find out what applies in your market. What directories are there? Make sure you are listed everywhere you can be listed for free, including your address, phone number, and website address.

In many directories, you can register to be found under certain keywords. Before you start paying for getting found for those words, make sure you get information from the listing company stating how many people actually use that keyword in search. They should be able to tell you this for a certain period, such as per month or year. If they can't tell you, they are probably not very good at what they do, and you are best to leave them alone. You don't want to pay money for listings if you have no way of evaluating whether are going to generate customers or not.

Within the marketing process, directory listings can help get **awareness**, as people will find you when looking for what you offer. When people find a complete and professional looking listing in a good directory, this will also build **trust**.

Logo

Your logo is not your brand, but it is a very important part of it. There are many things to take into consideration when designing a logo, and it is important to get a professional for the job. Your logo is the face of your company and often the first thing people see. It can have a major effect on how people see you, consciously or unconsciously. Your logo is important. Don't take it lightly. You are buying a face for your business. If you were really buying a face, you'd tread carefully, wouldn't you?

A strong logo can get people's attention and thereby create **awareness**, as well as interest. A logo can help get people to **like** and **trust** you, and a memorable and constantly visible logo is a strong reminder that can encourage **repeat sales**.

For a further discussion on logos, please refer to *Branding Untangled.*

Marketing Copy (or Text)

Your marketing copy, or marketing text, is extremely important. There are quite a few things to consider, such as what copy you need to have on hand and how it should be written. Here are some examples of the types of marketing copy you may need:

- Website copy
- Brochure copy
- Social media profile information
- Blog posts
- News releases
- Various promotional copy
- Case studies
- Frequently asked questions (FAQ)
- Sales copy
- and more...

Marketing copy is relevant in all stages of the marketing process. Good copy and content can do it all and some:

- It will get you noticed and get people's *interest*
- Can get people to *like* you
- Can build *trust*
- Can *sell*
- Can *sell again*
- Can help *referrals*—for example, when people have a look at your business card, brochure, website, flyer, etc.

Marketing Plan

A marketing plan includes all the details of your marketing strategy and program. It includes information about:

- Your market
- Your target groups
- Your competition
- Your brand strategy
- Which marketing activities will be used—your marketing program
- Project plan and budget for your marketing activities

This ensures that you have a clear plan to build your marketing on, and it makes sure that everyone on the team is on the same page and knows where you are heading.

Most of the above is covered in the *Marketing Untangled* Series, apart from analysing your market (although it might be an idea to do one about that. :)) The series also doesn't cover project plans and budgets in any detail, except for how to use them to make sure you can get your marketing activities done, i.e., set up a marketing system. Internet search will give you a lot of great resources about project management and budgeting, which is not just relevant for your marketing, but for your business as a whole.

Name

> *"Name creation is too important to be relegated to a brainstorming session among a few insiders around a kitchen table or in an executive lunchroom ... a name is much more permanent than most other elements of a marketing program..."*
>
> — David A. Aaker[14]

The name of your business, product, or service might be the only thing people see or hear of it for a long time. As soon as they hear or see it, it evokes mental and emotional connections, even though they may be hearing or seeing it for the first time, and the word as such has no actual meaning (think Kodak, Google, or Ikea). A name is, therefore, an extremely important marketing asset, and there are a lot of things that need to be considered when choosing a name. Just a few things to mention are memorability, spelling, how it translates into other languages, mental associations, trademark law, whether a suitable URL is available and so much more. It's not as simple as it may seem, so I recommend you get help from someone who has experience with finding brand names. It could save you a lot of money and headaches down the road.

A good name can help get people's **interest** and **awareness** for your business, product, or service. A good name can also help make your brand **like**able, **trust**worthy, and memorable.

Search Engine Optimisation (SEO)

Search Engine Optimisation (SEO) is all about getting found at or toward the top of online search results when people are looking for products and services such as those you offer. It can be incredibly valuable for your business to be at the top of the search results for the right keywords (see previous discussion of keyword analysis).

Generally speaking, if you optimise for Google, you tend to do well on the other main search engines, such as Yahoo and Bing.

SEO is, however, not just for your website. It can often be easier to rank for your social media profiles. Just try doing a search on Google for your name. Your Facebook or LinkedIn profiles (if you have them) are likely to be the top results because these websites are already so strong in the search results. It is, therefore, also important to optimise your social media profiles for search, because they may give you a better opportunity of getting found online than your website, and from there, you can then lead people to your website or your door.

SEO is quite a lot of work, and it is never ending work. It is not something you just do once and then never again. I often get clients asking about SEO work, thinking it is a package that they can buy once and that's it. That is by no means true. There are some fundamental things that need to be done at the beginning, hard core practical things, such as onsite optimisation tasks like your "page title" and "page description" and other *fun* things like that. But today SEO is less and less techie and more and more about core marketing things, such as content marketing and social media activity. SEO is, therefore, an ongoing thing you need to nurture.

Learning the basics of SEO may be more than enough for some to do it themselves. This can particularly apply for local search, i.e., getting found in your local area, rather than internationally. For those who need to enlist help from the experts, it is still important to get a basic understanding of what SEO involves, so you can better work with the experts and be an informed buyer.

As with keyword analysis, SEO is important to get **awareness** online. When people search for your kind of products or services, good SEO will result in them discovering you. As with keyword analysis, you can also say that being at the top of the search results helps build **trust** in your business, as people tend to think that Google would not rank you this high if you were not doing something right. ;)

Social Media

I have yet to find a business that cannot benefit from the use of some social media platform. Therefore, they definitely belong in Priority 1. However, as I mentioned before, there are so many of them, I felt they deserved a section of their own, which you will find later in the book. ;)

Website

Your website is definitely a core tool in your marketing. People will use it to get information about your business, products, and services. Very often, people don't contact your business until they are quite a long way through the marketing process, and a lot of the work involved in leading them *through* that process can take place on your website. It is, therefore, important to ensure that your website has all the information people need when they are considering purchasing your products and services.

There are many things to consider when it comes to your website, and good preparation on your part, before going to your website designer, can save you money, time, and headache. Preparations include being clear about the purpose of your website, having considered its structure and layout, as well as its content.

Your website can't ever be the tool that gets awareness or initial interest in the marketing process. People need to know about it and be interested in checking it out before ever getting to it. In other parts of the lead management system it is, however, very important and can work very hard for you.

Your website can help get people to **like** and **trust** you in a variety of ways:

- A professional looking website that is "on brand" will positively affect visitors and build trust.

- Good website copy (the text on the website) can have a positive impact and build trust and likeability, both with regard to content and tone of voice.

- Content is crucially important. Give your visitors whatever they need to make a decision to buy from you. Help them in whichever way you can. This will show them that you know your stuff, tell them what you are about, and it can build trust and likeability.

- Let them see the people behind the business. People do business with people, not faceless businesses, and people want to know the people they are doing business with. Have photos of your staff, and, if relevant, information about things like education and experience in their field to build trust. Giving insight into their personalities and daily life also makes them more relatable and helps build likeability and trust.

- Your website can help the *trial* part of the process. You want to have as much good information about your products or services as possible. Make sure you have good photos, product and service descriptions, etc. If you are worried about giving your competition too much information about what you do, err on the side of the potential customer. If the customer does not get the information they need from you, they might not bother to make the effort to contact you for it, and may look elsewhere, particularly if your competitors are more forthcoming.

- A clear return policy can help in the trial part of the process, as people realise that they can return the product if they are not happy, thereby reducing perceived risk. With services, consider how you can use the website to give people a taste of what they will get, using things like descriptions, outlining processes, photos, videos, testimonials, etc.

- You can definitely *sell* through your website; and if the product is digital, it can even be delivered through it. If you are selling through your website, you need to take great care to make that process as smooth as possible. A few things to consider are:

  o Making sure the sales process is simple and transparent.

  o Making sure that the customer can get assistance, if needed, as soon as possible and through the communication channel of choice (email, telephone, online chat, etc.).

  o Accepting all major credit cards and PayPal.

  o Showing that payment processing is secure through verifications and such (crucial for trust).

○ Possibly offering other forms or types of payments, such as bank transfers or other ways that are appropriate in your market.

You can use your website to encourage **repeat sales** through various ways. Here are a few ideas:

- By providing your customers with useful and interesting content on your website, you can encourage repeat visits.

- Offer your customers an appropriate addition to what they have already bought by featuring them with the main product (add-ons or up-sells). Classic examples would be batteries with battery-operated equipment, an extra lens for that camera, and such. Make them feel special by giving them the insider deal and VIP treatment.

- Having good guides, information, and instructions about your product or service on your website encourages repeat visits and, therefore, repeat contact with your business, increasing the likelihood of further purchases. Consider what your customers may want and need after they purchase and give them that to keep them coming back.

- Based on the customer's previous purchase, offer them other things that they may be interested in (which you know, based on what you know about them already ;)). Amazon is obviously an excellent example of how this is done but small businesses can do a lot more of this than you might think without breaking the bank.

Your website is crucial when it comes to **referrals**. More often than not, the first thing people do when they hear about something is to look for it online and check out the website.

Make sure that the great introduction you already got from the referral is not wasted by ruining it once people check out the site. People are often quite far along in the marketing process when they come to your site if they have been referred to you, so you should be able to close that sale if your website does its job. ;)

When it comes to your website, there are a lot of things to consider, so I suggest you get a professional for the job. There are, however, lots of things that you can and should have prepared and things you can do to ensure that the project comes in sooner and more affordable than if you don't, and it just makes the whole project easier. Good preparation pays off.

Your Network

Your network is one of your most powerful marketing tools. The mistake we too often make is not building it in a focused and efficient way. You need to make sure you nurture and manage your network so you can get as much as possible out of it.

May I suggest you write down the names and details of everyone you know who may be of any help whatsoever to your business or projects. Who they are will depend on you and your business. This can be computer and technology savvy people who may be able to advise or help you with things like your website or Facebook. They may be graphic designers or people who work for big business and may be able to help you get business there or can introduce you to the right people. They could be buyers in the stores where you want to sell your products, people in the media, bloggers, or people who can introduce you to people like that. These people might be experts and professionals you could collaborate with in your marketing and content marketing, who can guest post for you, write eBooks, know how to do webinars, etc. (See also content marketing and marketing partnerships later in this book.)

Mapping your network in a mind map is a good idea. You could get someone you know to help you map this, such as your partner, best friend, or a former colleague—they might remember someone or notice a connection that you may not have seen.

Also map those people that you want to get in touch with. These can be specific people (Joe Jones, HR manager for Scoobydoo, Inc.) or "someone who can help me with Facebook ads." Then look at how you can reach that person—who do you know who knows Joe and would be willing to introduce you?

In your map, you may find it helpful to colour code. Those you already know could be a neutral colour, such as black, those you are getting to know could be green, and those you want to connect with could be pink. The mission then is to find the connection with the pink ones and figure out ways you can establish connections.

See if you can find these people on social media. Start following them where appropriate (do not send them a friend request on Facebook unless you know them but do follow them if they have this enabled). Like their updates, comment, etc., to get on their radar and start building a relationship.

Let technology help you manage this. You can do this through simple tools like your online contacts directory, but tools like CRM systems are constantly getting simpler to use and many of them are free for basic usage (CRM stands for Customer Relationship Management). A CRM system can help you keep track of all communication with individual people and will remind you of your next meeting and when you should pick up the phone or send them an email. These tools also ensure that no matter who in your business is talking to that individual, they always know exactly what is going on as all the information is in the system. This can be a very useful tool to master.

When hearing the word "networking," many people cringe. They may find it uncomfortable and don't like the idea of getting to know people in order to establish business connections. They might feel that others must see through them and think the only reason they are talking to them is to benefit from it. I totally understand. I also struggle with this.

Things changed, however, when I realised I was looking at this in completely the wrong way. Now, instead of approaching networking by thinking about how I can benefit from getting to know the person in question, I think about it from the other way around: What can I do for others? What can I give to them?

Amazing things happen when you start to look at networking in this way. Get people to tell you what they do and what they need. Help them whenever you can. Connect them with other people—think how this person can help your customers. People will be attracted to you and will want to reciprocate.

Also, don't always be thinking about business. Just get to know people on a personal level. Talk about things you may have in common, like soccer, golf, kids, or whatever you find. Start there, and then develop and nurture the relationship. Business will follow much more easily.

Do a thorough analysis of your network and review it at least once a year. Set goals for nurturing your network. For example, you can have a goal of meeting two new people per month, or every month contacting two people you already know to maintain and nurture a relationship that is already established.

Use LinkedIn to build and maintain your network (see more in the section on social media).

As you already know, referrals are a really powerful marketing tool, and your network is a big part of getting those and thereby influencing the whole marketing process.

Priority 2: Marketing Activities You Must Use but Not Until After Priority 1!

Brand Guide

A brand guide (often also called style guide or design guide) is a document portraying the brand strategy and system, and guidelines regarding the brand identity design and brand tone of voice. It should include your brand strategy, set forward in a simple and easy to understand manner, detailed information about the brand system, and a design standard explaining which colours to use (in all colour systems), what fonts, font sizes in things such as headlines, body copy, etc., as well as rules regarding the use of your logo and guidelines and instructions regarding your brand tone of voice.

Your brand guide ensures consistency in the look and feel of everything that comes from your brand, at every touchpoint, whether it is in the way things look or its tone, to ensure that whoever is working with the brand is clear on what they can and cannot do, because they have a clear framework and rules.

In the future, you will work with a lot of different people on building your brand and representing it. These could be graphic designers, advertising agency people, designers, architects, photographers, printers, etc. If they don't know exactly what brand you want to build, how it should be represented, and if they don't understand it, they are not going to be able to help you build it. And if you don't have any guidelines, you will have a very hard time ensuring the consistency of your brand identity.

Your brand and brand identity play a vital role in the marketing process, getting you noticed, arousing people's **interest**, and building **likeability** and **trust**. A consistent look and feel also makes you memorable, reminding people of your brand each and every time they come into contact with it, however small that contact may be.

The brand guide was discussed in detail in a previous book in the *Marketing Untangled Series: Branding Untangled: The Small Business & Entrepreneur's Guide to Branding Your Business,* so if you want to delve deeper, I suggest you grab a copy. ;)

Content Marketing

Content marketing is something that many businesses are using today, although some may not be aware of it. If you are using any of the following in your marketing, there is content marketing involved:

- Any form of social media
- Blog
- Emails
- Newsletters
- Articles
- Videos
- eBooks
- Digital magazines
- Infographics
- Webinars
- Podcasts
- Vlogs (video blogs)
- Print magazine / newsletter
- Case studies

- White papers
- Free reports
- Cheat sheets
- Mind maps
- Swipe files
- Toolkits
- Resource lists
- Templates
- Quizzes or surveys
- Events
- Demos
- Free trials
- Spec sheets
- Mini classes
- And more...

Marketing today is more and more about producing, curating, and sharing content that people are interested in and has value for them, but at the same time is working for you by building **awareness**, **interest**, **likeability**, and **trust**, as well as encouraging **repeat** business and **referrals**. Search engine optimisation and overall awareness building online (and arguably offline) is more and more about producing and publishing good content, making content marketing more important than ever.

What should I post on Facebook, Twitter, LinkedIn, Pinterest, etc.? What should I blog about, and what should I say in my emails? How can I make this interesting and of value to my target audience, while also marketing my business and getting it to help make sales? How can I create this content? How can I do all this without drowning in work?! These are all marketing issues that businesses today face, and they constitute content marketing.

Content marketing can cover all parts of the marketing process, based on what you are talking about and which medium you use. As an example, using social media to promote great free content can get you **awareness** and **interest** (lead generation) and then people have to sign up to your mailing list to get the content (lead capture). By using emails, you can nurture the relationship and build that **like** and **trust** factor, show them that you really know your stuff, and give people a good idea of what you have to offer, thereby covering the **trial** part of the process (lead nurture).

Useful content designed specifically for your customers can also help **repeat sales** and help them **refer** more business to you (ongoing lead management). Think about what kind of content you need and what medium for that content may be right for your market.

Customer Testimonials

Get testimonials from your customers, with permission to use them in your marketing. It's even better if those customers are some well-known businesses or people.

Testimonials are more effective if you can publish them with the customer's name and photo—even better, get them on video. Some get people to do a short video message (you can simply record it with a good smartphone) and put it online and on social media.

People like to see testimonials to be assured that they are buying the right thing. It's a form of social proof.

For some kinds of businesses, having a customer list on their websites can work, as well. This is more applicable in B2B markets, but it can also be used in B2C. You have most likely seen logos from well-known businesses featured on websites as social proof. You will need to get approval from the businesses in question before listing them. This is not quite as strong as getting a quote, but this is still quite effective and can be simpler to do.

A customer list shows that you do already have customers and people who have put their trust in you before, and it acknowledges the work you have done. Each time you work for someone worth putting on the list, ask for their permission and then add them if permission is granted.

Customer testimonials and lists will also help build your user image—the image people have of the sort of people or businesses that do business with you, which is a strong part of your brand image.

Don't be afraid to ask for that testimonial. Most people are more than willing if they are happy with your products or services, but this won't happen by itself. Set yourself a goal for gathering them. For example, as a rule, always ask for testimonials at the end of a seminar or any sort of relevant event. If you do project work, ask for a testimonial at the end of each project. You can also just have a regular point in time (once a month, once a quarter, etc.) when you contact customers to request testimonials, if the nature of your business does not lend itself to including it in a straightforward process. The best way to ensure you gather testimonials is to have a set process for how and when you do this, so you don't forget and to ensure that you get fresh new testimonials on a regular basis.

Use the testimonials everywhere you can, such as:

- On your website
- In social media
- Choose a testimonial each month and include it in your email signature
- In your marketing emails
- In print, where appropriate
- In advertising, where appropriate
- Etc.

Testimonials are always important, but in certain industries, they are absolutely crucial. As an example, reviews on sites such as TripAdvisor.com, booking.com, and hotels.com are key for the tourism industry and can greatly affect whether people buy or not.

You can also get reviews on Facebook, on your Google business listing (which also helps get you found on Google), on Yelp if you are in the US or UK, and on various other sites. Look into which sites are most applicable for your business and market. The key here is not just hoping that people give you a review or testimonial—ask for it!

If you provide a service, rather than a product, testimonials become even more important, because they help the *trial* part of the marketing process. As discussed previously, it is always harder to understand exactly what you are buying when buying a service than if you are buying a product, as you can't really return it for a refund (well, at least not a refund of the time you've put into trying it). Testimonials provide the social proof that reassures people they are making the right choice in buying that particular service, which thereby helps the sale.

Testimonials are *referrals* by nature, and as discussed previously, referrals are a powerful marketing tool that can work throughout the marketing process. Be organised and focused and ask for those testimonials. Don't just cross your fingers and hope for the best.

Getting Media Coverage

Media coverage can be an enormously powerful marketing tool. You may well be able to get it for free, making it a great option for small- and medium-sized businesses with a limited budget. To get it, however, you need to have a systematic approach to it.

Make a list of the media you would like to be featured in, the people within those media you want to get in touch with and consider what kind of story would be right for each medium. The key here is having a "hook" to the story—something that will interest people—and that also means interesting the editor or reporter in question. The fact that you came out with a new product or are having a sale won't be newsworthy and, therefore, will not be of much interest, but you may, for example, have an unusual or interesting story of how your product came about that a reporter might find worth telling.

I have had clients who get frustrated about having to find the right "angle," particularly when the most obvious angle is for them to share a personal story or experience and they are not up for it. Some feel like they are selling themselves; others don't mind sharing pieces of their personal lives. At the end of the day, the choice is yours. You can choose to use what you've got and get the story told, or you can choose not to.

Being ready to put yourself out there can be a great way to let the world know about you. After one of my clients went through a divorce, she took a long hard look at her life and decided it was time to take better care of herself. She lost a lot of weight and inspired a lot of people around her. Telling her story in a national women's magazine got her coverage that also featured her design work, which gave her business a great boost. Whatever you do, just make sure you are comfortable with it—and remember, it is *your* decision.

Like with so many other things in your marketing, getting media coverage is more about being organised in the way you go about getting it and doing the work, rather than being some sort of genius. Find the right media, the right people within it (the decision makers *and* the ones that cover the sort of topics appropriate for you), and the right story. Persistence, whilst also knowing when to stop, is also a good quality. ;)

Media coverage can cover many parts of the marketing process. It is through the media that we often first see or learn about something, thereby getting **awareness** and **interest** (lead generation).

Positive media coverage can help the *like* and *trust* factor, not just through what is being said, but also because people have a tendency to trust what they see in the media because it is assumed that journalists have vetted things before giving them coverage (lead nurturing).

Media coverage can often be the thing that nudges people to make a decision and take action, thereby encouraging the *purchase* (lead conversion) and acting as a reminder. Media coverage that discusses the product or service in question, or talks about customer experiences, can help bring people through the *trial* part of the process.

As your customers see you in media and learn about new products or services you are offering, you increase the likelihood of *repeat purchases*.

In some ways, media coverage, by its nature, is a *referral* tool, and it helps others refer business to you and gives you credibility. If that recommendation from Johnny is accompanied by, "Didn't you see them in the paper the other day?" or "Didn't you hear them on the radio this morning?" or something along those lines, it will carry more weight.

One thing to remember, though: Media is a marketing channel that is largely out of your control, and you also cannot guarantee consistent visibility with it. It should, therefore, never be the only marketing activity covering any single part of the marketing process as it is too unreliable for that. Consider it a supporting act—a bonus, if you will—one of those ladders up the board.

Good Photographs

Good photos matter. Don't just use images shot on your smartphone in your marketing materials, except perhaps in social media, if appropriate for your brand. Don't use poor quality photos or low resolution. For any print materials, the resolution should be no less than 300 dpi. Online images can have lower resolution but make sure they look good. Don't ever take a photo and enlarge it for use in large mediums, such as posters or full-page ads, if they do not have a high enough resolution. We've all seen those pixelated or stretched images at one time or another. It looks awful and will have a negative effect on your brand image.

Don't skimp here. It can easily be worth getting a professional photographer if you need photos. Good photos, with good subject materials, can do so much for your brand and give you a distinctive and interesting look that can take you far. The subject matter is, of course, also very important.

Stock photography is an option, and you can obtain them from an array of websites. They can be great, but it should always be kept in mind that these images are not specific to you and they tend to have that "stock photo flavour," particularly if they have people in them. They are not special in any way, and anyone can use them (if you want to buy a license to use them exclusively, this is crazy expensive, and territory limited). Most people can easily spot stock photos from a mile away, consciously or unconsciously, and they will affect your brand, more often than not in a negative way. Some research has even indicated that using stock photos can have an expressly negative effect.[15] People can see that this is not a real person from that particular business, but just a typical stock photo model.

I'm not saying that you shouldn't use stock photos at all; after all, professional and original photos cost a pretty penny. I am merely saying use them well and be aware of the pitfalls. ;)

Don't ever use photos that you don't have permission to use. If you have taken the photos yourself, you will need permission from any people in the photos before you can use them. Under no circumstances can you just go online, find a photo, and use it. Trust me. I have known people who have been slapped with a huge fine because they used photos they did not have permission to use, and there is nothing you can do but pay up.

There are websites where you can find images you can use for free, in some cases and given some conditions, such as giving the owner expressed credit and such. If you use photos from sources like that, make sure you completely understand how things work, what you need to do to be able to use the photo, and adhere to the rules.

Have a look at photos all around you, online, in the media, in marketing materials, etc. I don't need to tell you how hugely important they are. It's evident. Photos can grab attention and get you **awareness** and **interest** (lead generation). They can clearly get people to **like** you through what they show and their feel. In and of themselves, good photos may not build **trust** (although they can), but you can be sure that bad photos can destroy trust.

Good product photos or photos from services or experiences can go a long way to get people through the **trial** part of the marketing process (just think online shopping ;)). Photos can help **repeat sales** and **referrals** by reminding your customers of what else you have to offer and help them in referring further business to you by showing your product or service (ongoing lead management).

Google Analytics

Google Analytics is a free website analytics tool from Google that you definitely should have connected to your website. Through Google Analytics, you can get a lot of information like:

- How many visitors you get to your website
- Where visitors to your website are coming from (channels such as Facebook, organic search, etc.)
- Which countries your visitors come from
- Which browser your visitors are using
- Which pages your visitors are looking at

- How long they are spending on those pages
- Whether visitors are new or returning
- Whether visitors are using desktop computers, tablets, or smartphones
- And a wealth of other information

You can set up more advanced measurements, such as for conversions (the percent of people who sign up on a given webpage, the percent of people who buy and such), tracking whether people go through processes you have set up (funnels), and a lot of other things. You can even set up your own dashboard of key performance indicators (KPIs) to check regularly and have the system send you regular reports.

Google Analytics has a wealth of possibilities. I have found that a lot of people do not use it as much as they should, and many not at all. It's quite understandable. If you are not used to things like this, it can be intimidating, and it can safely be said that the user interface isn't particularly intuitive. However, it's worth learning the basics to be able to measure the most important things for your business. Luckily, as this is a Google product, you will find a lot of great material online to help you learn how to use Google Analytics, whether you just want the basics or want to go more advanced.

Google My Business

Google My Business is the hub for your business on Google, giving you one place from which you can manage your online presence on this Internet behemoth. Your profile includes your business listing, which puts you on Google Maps and gets you those search results that show information about your business to the right of the search engine results when people look for your business specifically. The Google business listing is free, and it's definitely something you should use to the max as it helps you get found online.

Through the Google My Business dashboard, you can maintain up-to-date business information on Google, feature photos, get reviews, and much more. Google is constantly evolving this service, and you can even create a simple website and have it on your own domain!

How does Google My Business help in the marketing process? It can help in various ways.

With a good profile, linking to your website, social media, and online profiles, you increase your chances of getting found online and gaining **awareness**. With the right information, good copy, and images, Google My Business can help increase **interest** and **like**ability (lead generation and nurture). The right information can build **trust** (lead nurture), and content and reviews can help the **trial** part of the process. Continued contact with customers (e.g., reviews) could help **repeat business** and attract **referrals** (ongoing lead management).

Google Search Console

Google Search Console is yet another great free offering from Google that can help your marketing. At the very least, you should register your website in the console, put your sitemap in there, and make sure Google has indexed your website to increase the likelihood of it being found. The tool offers a lot of other possibilities to improve your online presence. The Console also monitors your website's health and can alert you of errors, speed problems, and lots more.

The best way to get started is simply to do a Google search for how to set up Google Search Console for your type of content management system, e.g., WordPress, Squarespace, etc. You should easily be able to find good instructions online. ;)

Since Google Search Console can help your website get found online, as well as make sure it is working as well as it can, this is a tool which helps *awareness* and can affect other parts of the marketing process by improving your website overall.

Market and Marketing Research

Market and marketing research are a crucial part of your marketing. The scope and execution depend on your needs at each time, which can vary greatly. You can research the market, such as your target audience, competition, or market environment (market research), and you can do research related to your marketing activities (marketing research). This can include things like testing of products and services in development, testing various marketing communications methods, analysing results, customer surveys, and a variety of other things.

When starting out or running a small- or medium-sized business, research can seem overwhelming. However, you can do simple and cost-effective research; and I recommend you do that, even if just to get indications. You may not have the capacity to do research that would stand up to academic rigour, but even fairly basic research can be helpful, and knowing something is better than knowing nothing at all.

The fact is that no one can read minds, despite all the films and TV shows showing otherwise. It is important that we don't make assumptions. Do some research and work with facts, not fiction. There is a phrase I am very fond of: if you assume, you are only making an "ASS-of-U-and-ME." Don't assume that you know what your customers want or think—find out. Don't assume that there is a market for your product or service—find out. Decca, Columbia, and others did not sign the Beatles, saying they'd never amount to anything, and someone is supposed to have said that Fred Astaire could not sing or act and could only dance a little! Boy, did their assumptions cost them, and they totally made an ass of themselves!

There are lots of different ways to do research, the details of which are outside the scope of this book. Here are just a few ideas to get you going:

Secondary research (also referred to as desk research) involves examining data and information that already exists. If there is one thing there seems little lack of in the 21st century, it's information. The Internet is a treasure trove, but you will need to be critical of what you find to ensure that you are using valid and up-to-date information. You will also find that you have a lot of useful information inside your business, such as sales figures, accounting records, client information and more. Starting with secondary research can save you time and money and help you define what additional information, if any, you may require.

Primary research can be more tailored to your needs than desk research. Scope creep is, however, always a danger, and you need to be very organised and efficient to get good information and avoid things getting out of hand. The methods you use depends on your resources and the information you are after. Here are a few:

- Online surveys
- Field research, where you go out and talk to people
- Focus groups
- Interviews
- Information from your customer service staff
- Phone, mail, or email surveys (note that you need permission before you contact people for this type of research)
- Purchase research reports

Remember to only gather the information you need. It's easy to spend unnecessary time and energy and end up with the all too common condition of analysis paralysis, where you simply get lost in a flood of information. It can also be a challenge to determine what exactly it is you need to research in order to get the information and answers you need. Have clear goals for your research and stay on task.

Marketing Partnerships

Marketing partnerships are all about working with other businesses who share your target group(s) but do not compete with you. By working together, you join your resources and have the potential to get much better results than you can on your own, making this a win-win for both parties. There are few, if any, businesses that cannot in some way benefit from partnering with others in their marketing.

A good way to find potential partners is to ask your current customers which other businesses they do business with—and are happy with. You only want to work with the best ;)

Here are a few examples and ideas for things to collaborate on:

Use your content marketing!

A personal trainer could create an eBook on how to prevent sore shoulder muscles by doing 10 minutes of the right exercises each day. The nutritionist he is collaborating with can then send this to her email list. The personal trainer gains subscribers to his list (if he requires people to sign up before they get the eBook), gets exposure to the nutritionist's audience, and shows his expertise and how helpful he is. At the same time, the nutritionist looks good by giving her audience additional content that they are interested in and can benefit from.

The nutritionist could then do an eBook about all the best supplements to combat stress, and the personal trainer shares this with his audience. As you can see, these two eBooks would be great for people like me and you who are busy and probably do way too much work at the computer. ;)

A business financial advisor could invite her clients to a short seminar with a marketing consultant. The marketing consultant gets visibility with the financial advisor's clients, and the financial advisor looks good by giving her clients this free seminar. This can then be done the other way around.

In general, trading content like this, in whichever format (books, videos, seminars, workshops, etc.) is great. It gives visibility to the business creating the content, and the business giving this to their audience gets brownie points for giving them something of value.

Special Deals

A hair salon could give every customer discount coupons for the beauty salon next door, encouraging the customer to go to that beauty salon where they can try their services. This gives the beauticians a chance to sweep the salon's customers off their feet and gain a long-term customer. And, as I am sure you thought of already, vice versa ;)

Another example could be that when you book a table at a restaurant for Valentine's dinner, you get a coupon for the florist—or a free rose if only you pick it up at the florist. The restaurant looks good (let's face it, who can't use a little help with romance ;)), this brings you to this particular florist, and you will like them for doing this for you. As a result, you are likely to go there the next time you need flowers. In reverse, when you buy flowers for a certain amount at the florist, you get a coupon for free dessert at the restaurant. :)

Remember, people need to get something that has value. If the deal looks cheap, it could actually do more harm than good to your image. ;)

Be active in referring business to your marketing partners. If you do, they are more likely to refer business to you. Referring your customers to someone who they are then happy with gets you a few bonus points with the customers, as well. ;)

Do business with your marketing partners. This not only makes you a more credible referrer, but you can also give them a customer testimonial to use on their website, in social media, and in other appropriate places and they are then, again, more likely to reciprocate.

Marketing partnerships can be a great tool for the marketing process. By getting exposure through your partners, you get **awareness** sooner than with many other methods. The audience is also more likely to be *interested* in you. If not, you've probably not picked the right partner. ;) You also borrow *like*ability and *trust* from your partners and may reduce the importance of *trial* before purchase. Marketing partnerships can, therefore, be a great lead management tool.

Priority 3: Marketing Activities You May Want to Use

Autoresponders or Automated Emails

Automated emails, or autoresponders, are emails programmed to be sent automatically, triggered by certain actions. This can be simple things like sending a birthday greeting if people have given you their birthdate, getting a certain email once you have made a purchase (also called transactional emails), or simply emails sent a certain amount of time after a previous email was sent. Depending on the sophistication of your email service, you can even have an email triggered if people click a certain link in your last email, visit a certain webpage of yours, or simply when they sign up for your email list. There is a wealth of possibilities with this!

Automatic emails can be an online marketer's dream and biggest helper. Triggering a specific sequence of emails to build a relationship with your subscribers can improve your lead nurturing, as well as save you a ton of time and headache. You can set up an elaborate sequence of emails personalised and designed to fit exactly what your subscribers need to in order to make up their mind and make a purchase. As you can imagine, this is a great way to automate and optimize your lead nurturing process, as well as ongoing lead management.

If you are planning to use email marketing (which I generally recommend you do), and if you are going to do proper online marketing, you are more likely than not to want to use automatic email. Automatic emails are something you simply have to learn to use.

Blog

Blogging is a powerful marketing tool in so many ways. It can be the heart of your content marketing, and an active, well written blog with good usage of keywords can really help search engine optimisation (SEO) and drive traffic to your website.

However, blogging is not enough on its own. You need to do a lot more than just write for blogging to work for you. You need to blog regularly, the content needs to be of top quality, and the blog needs to be promoted. Don't decide to blog unless you are ready to do it at least once a week, and preferably two or three times to get results. We all know how sad it is to see a website with the last entry being a few months old. You can't help but think that the business is about to close or something!*

A lot of the things written about content marketing above applies to blogging. A good blog post can go viral and gain **awareness** and **interest** (lead generation). Good content builds **like**ability and **trust** and builds your reputation as an expert in your field (lead nurturing).

Blogging used with email marketing is a powerful combo, and it can also help to continue your relationship with your customers and encourage both **repeat sales** and **referrals** (ongoing lead management).

* Full disclosure: As I now do less consulting and, therefore, don't market myself as much as I did before, I am very guilty of this! :)

Case Studies

Case studies are really just stories about your customers and the results they received from using your product or service. A case study is not just a great way to get a recommendation for your product or service, but when others can relate to the people or businesses in the case studies, whose problems are solved, the cases become an even stronger marketing tool.

To be effective, the story needs to include:

- Where are the customers before coming to you, and what is their situation?
- What is the problem they have?
- What is the solution you are providing?
- Concrete, measurable results.

As with customer testimonials, if you can do case studies with known individuals or businesses, they become even stronger.

Case studies have more credibility if published with the name of the customer or the customer's business. In B2B, also publishing the name, job title, and photo of a representative of the business is strong, as well. The case study can be presented as text, or it can even be done as a video. It is always good to visually represent data, particularly if you are communicating a lot of figures and statistics, so keep that in mind.

If you choose to do case studies, set a goal to do them on a regular basis. If you do project work, make this something you always do at the end of a successful project. You can also just do them at regular intervals, like every three months or so.

Case studies are by their very nature a **referral**, as with testimonials. They have the potential to get people through the whole marketing process and can be quite powerful.

Case studies as marketing tools are at their strongest when people are getting close to the sale, i.e., to build **trust** and cover the **trial** part of the process. They are not as effective as a first touchpoint, simply because they will take time to read or watch, so people are probably not willing to spend the time until they are further along in the marketing process.

Email Marketing

In this day and age of social media, people regularly chime in, saying that email is dying. They could not be more wrong. At the time of this writing, multiple sources cite email as giving the highest return on marketing investment, and it shows no signs of waning. Building your email list is one of the best things you can do in your marketing, and even better is using it to its utmost—in the right way!

Why is email such a good marketing tool? Well, the fact that people have subscribed means they have given you permission to send them email, straight to their inbox. There are no algorithms anywhere deciding whether people will see your message or not (as with Facebook, for example), and you don't need to pay through the nose each and every time you want to contact your subscribers. Bringing people from your emails to your website does not require fancy SEO tactics, just simply good content and giving them what they are interested in with clear calls to action and a link. And even if people don't read each and every one of your emails, they are constantly being reminded of you as they see your email in their inbox.

There are a number of things that need to be kept in mind with regard to email marketing. This could easily be the subject of its own book. What I must stress here is that you learn about using email marketing before you start, including things such as rules and regulations (e.g. GDPR and the CAN-SPAM act) and best practices. This is not only a question of ethics, but also simply a question of effectiveness. Email marketers that don't adhere to the rules can quickly find their deliverability rates dropping or, even worse, have their domain blacklisted, and reversing those sorts of actions is no laughing matter.

Email marketing is an important part of content marketing and online marketing in general, and far too often it is only used to send promotional offers and adverts, when it can be a great way to build a long-term relationship. Once you have people on your list, you can really start building a relationship with them, getting them to **like** you and **trust** you. This is probably one of the best lead nurturing tools out there. This is a great tool to continue your relationship with your customers and get **repeat sales**, and it can help **referrals** both through content and through people forwarding emails to friends (ongoing lead management).

I cannot stress enough how powerful email marketing can be for your business and how important it is that you learn how to use it well.

Follow-up Offers

Once people have bought from you, they are often open to buying more. So, get them while they are in that frame of mind and send them a follow-up offer right after the initial sale. It's best if the offer is in some way related to the initial purchase.

As an example, if someone has just bought a fairly expensive camera, send them an offer for an extra lens, or an extra memory card or battery. Someone who just bought your web design services could well be open to SEO services or social media training. Think of ways you could use this tactic.

This is obviously a tool to get a **repeat sale** from your existing customers. ;)

Free Webinars

A webinar is an online event that is broadcast to people through their computers via the Internet. It is sometimes also called a "webcast," "online event," or "web seminar."

Free webinars can be a powerful marketing tool. They are part of your content marketing, and you can have them either live or recorded. They can be a lead magnet for your email list (see more about lead magnets below) or just useful and interesting content on your website, YouTube, or other social media. Webinars are a great way to build your reputation as an expert by showing people what you've got, and they are an effective way to build a strong relationship with your target audience.

I am listing free webinars as a marketing tool, but webinars—essentially live online classes—can, of course, be a product in and of themselves. You can sell them, giving your business another revenue stream. This is definitely something that is worth checking out.

Webinars can be great for **interest** (lead generation), and they build **like**ability as people get to know you through them and by giving valuable content. They can build **trust** by showing what you have to offer (lead nurturing) and can be a great way to get people through the **trial** part of the marketing process.

Webinars can be a great tool to get the **sale** (lead conversion), as well as a way to continue your relationship with your customers, thereby gaining **repeat sales**. They are great for **referrals**, as people encourage others to attend (ongoing lead management). As you can see, webinars are a great marketing tool, well worth checking out.

Google Ads

See also: Keyword Analysis, Pay-Per-Click Advertising, Search Engine Marketing

Google Ads (previously Google AdWords) is Google's advertising service. These are the text ads you see above and to the right of Google search results (see also search engine marketing or SEM), but they can also appear as banner ads on various other websites through their Google AdSense service. Google Ads are generally pay-per-click ads, although you can also pay per impression, i.e., how many people see your ads, even though they may not click them.

Google AdSense is the other side of the Google advertising coin. People with websites can show ads on their website through AdSense and get paid for that. I do not recommend you do this. You are running a business. You don't want to lead people away from your website by encouraging them to click on an ad for someone else. After all, you have done all the hard work to get them to your website so you can sell them your products and / or services (unless advertising revenue from AdSense is your business model, in which case you should know A LOT more about pay-per-click and Google Ads than the barebone basics I talk about in this book ;)).

Some SEO experts will recommend that you buy Google Ads, even if only for a small amount of money each month, as it will help you get found online. Even if it is only because as you buy the ad, Google crawls the site your ad leads to, and the more they crawl your site, the more they are aware of you and likelier to feature you in their results.

Growth Hacking

I had much debate with myself whether to include this in the book or not. However, with the concept becoming so widespread in marketing today, I thought it had to be covered for you to understand what it refers to (a lot of people throw the phrase around without seeming to really understand what it means).

So, what then is growth hacking?

Growth hacking is essentially a mindset. It refers to someone who is solely focused on growth (growth in revenue, growth in users, etc.) and not on the broader scope of marketing in the traditional sense. As the original growth hacker, Sean Ellis, put it, *"A growth hacker is a person whose true north is growth."*[16]

A growth hacker will look at the complete lead management process (also often referred to as a funnel) and find ways to increase results at each stage by creating hypotheses as to what might get better results, running experiments to see if it works, and optimising the results. Growth hackers use various tactics to get results. It's not the tactics used that make them a growth hacker. Tactics will change, there will always be new shiny things to use, and a good growth hacker often also uncovers tricks and tactics of their own. The whole thing is about the approach of iterating by analysing every step of the process, coming up with ideas for things that may get better results, and testing them. It's all about experimenting and then doing more of what works and stopping what doesn't work.

A reason I have a little bit of a problem with the term "growth hacking" is that too often the term is bandied about without people really knowing what it means. It should only be used for that role in the company that focuses solely on growth. In all our marketing, we should be coming up with ideas for improvements, testing them out, doing more of what works and not doing what doesn't work. We should always be applying this mindset to our business and our marketing: analysing, creating hypotheses, testing, optimising … it's just a commonsense way of doing business and marketing in this day and age. Throwing money at marketing tactics without having a way of knowing whether they really work is just … well, stupid. Yet people do it every day, particularly when using mainstream media such as TV, radio, and print, but no less with other tactics, such as Facebook or Google Ads.

Growth hacking applies to scalable digital products and services and is very much known as a startup term (although any business can use it). But humans can be incredibly creative, and many are finding ways to apply growth hacking thinking (as well as tools and tactics) in other areas, particularly to businesses that mix online and offline. Because a lot of growth hacking tactics often require technical skills (programming referral systems into software-as-a-service products, for example), a growth hacker needs to have a good understanding of technology. Although they don't need to be a programmer, they must be technically savvy and have the ability to work effectively with programmers and technical staff to implement their growth hacks. In a way, growth hacking is a bridge between the worlds of marketing and tech, and each tribe now has to understand the other in order to effectively work together and get results.

I hope this gives you some idea of what growth hacking is. In the reader resources at thoranna.is/mcureader, you will find links to some great content that delves deeper into growth hacking, if you want to learn more.

Landing Pages

Landing pages are often also called squeeze pages or opt-in pages, and sales pages are by their nature landing pages. In its purest sense, a landing page is any page on your website that people "land on" when they arrive on it. However, for the purposes of this discussion, a landing page is "a standalone web page distinct from your main website that has been designed for a single focused objective" (Unbounce.com).[17]

The point of a landing page is to get people to take a certain action—do a single thing. This could be signing up for your email list, registering for a webinar, buying, etc.

Landing pages are well researched marketing tools, and a wealth of tests has shown what works best to get people to do the one thing you want them to do on that page. One of the key elements that distinguishes a landing page from other pages on your website is that it has no navigation to anywhere else. You won't see the typical navigation bar across the top of the page. The point is that either people take the action you want them to take or they go away. There are no other options to choose from, which increases the likelihood of people taking the particular action you want them to take.

At a minimum, landing pages will have information about the offer in hand (here is my eBook, webinar, stuff, etc., this is what it is ...), and a sign-up form or a buy button. A landing page may also have other elements such as further product information, images, and forms of social proof, such as testimonials.

A good landing page is key in getting people onto the lead nurture stage in your lead management. This, along with your email sign-up form, is pure lead capture. *And* this is the tool that can clinch the **sale** online. The presentation and information on your landing pages need to build **like**ability and **trust** in order to get people to do what you want them to do, and information and testimonials need to help get people over the **trial** part.

Lead Magnet

A lead magnet is exactly what it says on the tin—a magnet to attract leads into your lead management system. Here's Digital Marketer's definition: "An irresistible bribe offering a specific chunk of value to a prospect in exchange for their contact information."[18] And it is the first step in your online lead management system.

You will most likely have come across a lead magnet online before. Some classic examples would be an eBook, a special report, a checklist, guide, cheat sheet, swipe files, templates, and toolkits. In any case, it is something people get for free when they sign up—and a brilliant way to get people to subscribe to your emails, that you then use to nurture the relationship. Hence, a lead magnet is the ultimate lead capture tool.

News on Your Website

Just like a blog, news on your website can be good for SEO by keeping the site active and by using the right keywords. This is also an opportunity to show your website visitors what your business is up to and tell them about projects, staff, new products, etc. Do keep in mind, though, that people are always interested in stuff that benefits *them*, rather than what you are up to, so it is questionable how much interest a self-centred news section could get. How many news feeds from companies do you follow? My guess is not many, unless perhaps you are investing in stocks. ;)

Just as with a blog, make sure you are ready to update your news section regularly, at least once a week. Seeing old news is not good and gives the impression that either you just can't be bothered, or worse, that there is nothing newsworthy going on in your business.

News has the potential to get **awareness** and **interest** (lead generation) and build **likeability** and **trust** (lead nurturing). News showing your product or service in action or that portrays happy customers can help the **trial** part of the process and **repeat sales** by reminding customers of you.

Pay-Per-Click Advertising (PPC)

See also: Google Ads, Keyword Analysis, Search Engine Marketing

Pay-Per-Click ads—or PPC—is an online advertising model where the advertiser pays each time a user clicks on their ad, and *only* when the ad is clicked.

There are a few different types of PPC ads and various platforms. The best-known platform is probably Google Ads, but PPC is also an element in ads on the large social media networks such as Facebook, Instagram, Twitter, YouTube, and LinkedIn. There are other PPC platforms, such as Bidvertiser, AdRoll, and BuySellAds, as well as the other large search engines, such as Bing.

The main types of PPC are search engine ads and banner ads. Probably the best-known examples of search engine ads are the ads that you see at the top and to the right of your Google search results, but you also get these on other search engines. These are primarily text based, although you can also have images.

Banner ads can appear pretty much all over the web. These are the image ads you'll see on various websites. Google Ads is also probably the best-known platform for these, and websites that are prepared to publish ads through the Google Ad platform can use the Google AdSense service to do so.

With PPC, you are paying to be found for certain keywords. How much you pay depends on how many others are paying to be found for that same keyword. What you essentially have is live bidding between competitors for being seen in relation to the keywords bid. Therefore, your competition directly affects your ads and their cost. There are other factors that come into play, such as how relevant the ad platform deems your ad to be to appear before the audience for a particular placement, and how valid the ad is, but this is the oh-so-very-simple explanation of how it works.

A few points to keep in mind when using PPC:

- Make sure you have clearly defined targets.
- Have a really good list of keywords.
- Know your competition like the back of your hand—they are the ones you are bidding against.
- Make sure to measure your results from the start—you don't want to be wasting money on things that don't work, and if you find things that work, you want to do more of those.
- Keep finetuning your campaign, and your knowledge of how this whole thing works. ;)

Using PPC ads on platforms such as Google Ads may *seem* simple, but it's very easy to flush money down the drain. I remember talking to a potential client who had spent well over $200 thousand over a three-month period with Google, with absolutely nothing to show for it.

Personally, I never recommend to my clients that they manage their own PPC campaigns, even on seemingly user-friendly platforms like Google Ads. Always enlist the services of PPC specialists, but as always, it's good to be familiar with how things work, so you can be an informed buyer of their services. Make sure you get regular result reports. After an initial period of setup and finetuning, your PPC expert should be able to guarantee that you at least break even on your PPC investment and preferably have a positive return on investment. How long until you can expect that is hard to say, though, as there are so many variables affecting the process. Just be sure to monitor things carefully—as I said, it's easy to throw money away.

Generally speaking, adverts are great for **awareness** and **interest** (lead generation) and can influence **like**ability and **trust**. They can also help **repeat sales** (ongoing lead management). Through retargeting (see more on that below), you can also advertise only to those who have already been to your website or interacted with your content on various social media, thereby getting increased exposure to people who have already expressed their interest by checking you out.

Point-of-Sale Marketing Materials

Point-of-sale (POS) marketing materials are just that, marketing materials used where the sale takes place. Think custom-made stands for products and signs in shop shelves—they are just a tiny example. When it comes to POS, there is a wealth of possibilities and no way to cover them all here. If this is applicable to your business, it is, however, important that you consider this carefully and thoroughly examine how you can get the most out of your POS marketing. How can you best bring attention to your product or service where it is sold?

Take a look at what others are doing for ideas and learn from the good and the bad. Should your products have a special display stand? Could you have a dangler or some signage on the shelf? Do you have a shop-in-shop sort of thing, that allows for more scope for impact? Of course, any POS materials need to be used in consultation with the owner of the retail space (if that's not you). Also, remember to think outside the box! Creative and interesting displays are likelier to grab attention and get people to check things out.

POS marketing is well known in fast moving consumer goods, as well as cosmetics and alcohol displays. Perhaps you are in an industry where they are not used that much, but could they be? Could they be an interesting new way to get people's attention?

POS materials can be all sorts, and creative people are constantly coming up with new and interesting ideas. Good POS materials can clearly get your product **awareness** and **interest**. If they are good and even clever, they can help the **like**ability factor and build **trust**. Information displayed at POS could even help the **trial** part of the marketing process.

Promotional and Booking Sites in Your Industry

If your industry has any websites that people visit to get information and find things, you should definitely look into listings on those. This applies to various industries, with tourism services being a classic example.

For example, if you provide accommodation, you should definitely have a good listing on TripAdvisor and possibly on sites such as booking.com or hotels.com

You should also be listed on sites for your area, such as local area promotional sites. In Iceland, for example, there are sites for various different geographic areas such as traveleast.is, visitreykjavik.is, visitreykjanes.is, and such. If there are sites like this for your area, look into getting listed on those.

If the sites charge for listing, make sure you get good information before paying up. How much traffic do they get? Who are their visitors? How many searches were done on the site in the past year for things such as those you are offering? How many bookings resulted (conversion rate)? If they don't get that much traffic from the right people or people are not searching for the kind of thing you offer, you will want to think carefully before you register. Is it worth it?

If you do decide to register, monitor what you are getting out of it and make sure you use your listing to its utmost potential. Have all the information necessary, ensure you are using the right keywords to get found, have good photos, etc.

Being where people search for things can get you the **awareness** you are looking for. SEO for your own website can be a lot of work in a competitive market, but big websites with a lot of good information will have an advantage when it comes to SEO. Sometimes it's just best to let those big sites do their work in pulling in people and then make sure you have a fantastic profile on there that makes people choose you above the others once they're in.

Make sure your profile and information get people's **interest** and get them to **like** and **trust** you. Testimonials and reviews can help build trust and get people through the **trial** part of the process, as well as being a potential **referral** in and of itself. **Sales** are often processed directly from these types of sites.

Public Speaking

Public speaking in various forms can be a great marketing tool for many businesses. If this is something you feel comfortable doing or have someone in your business who would be good at public speaking, this may be an option you want to explore for your marketing.

Some people build their careers on public speaking *and* get well paid for it. You may not be considering a paid speaker career, but still want to use it for marketing purposes. Speaking for free for the right audience can be a great way to get **awareness** and **interest** and build **like**ability and **trust**. This is also something that can work well in marketing partnerships, as discussed previously.

With public speaking, people who may not have seen you before are getting to know you, often because someone they know and trust has brought them to the talk or recommended you. This means they will notice you—et voilà: awareness. Through what you say and how you present yourself, you have an opportunity to interest them and get them to like and trust you. You get a chance to show just how good you are at what you do, or how good your business is at what it does, and you may even be able to cover things that help the **trial** part of the marketing process.

It is not uncommon for **sale**s to be generated at public speaking gigs (lead conversion). In my experience and that of many of my colleagues, a lot of business comes from people who have seen us speak somewhere. When your customers hear you speak, this also continues your relationship with them, which may lead to **repeat sales**. Encourage those customers and your business network to bring people to the event and turn it into a powerhouse of a **referral** tool. ;)

Referrals

We all know how great it is when we have happy customers who tell others about us. Those who hear of us in this way are much likelier than others to do business with us than those who find us through other channels. We also know that referrals are one of the few marketing tools that can cover every part of the marketing process, even without any help from any other marketing efforts.

Every business, product, or service can benefit from referrals in one way or the other, but, generally, the more expensive the purchase is or the more personal, the more important referrals become. Most of us will, for example, seek referrals when we look for a doctor, hairdresser, or private trainer, not to mention a realtor.

Organic "word-of-mouth" is one kind of referral, but there are also many ways that you can ask for and encourage referrals, thereby increasing them. Why just cross your fingers and hope someone recommends you when you can do things to make it happen? ;)

Many find asking for referrals uncomfortable. They may even feel like they are begging. The fact is, however, that if you have a good product or service that your customer is happy with, they are usually more than willing to tell others about it. Many also like recommending products and services they like to others, seeing it as a gift they are giving by helping them out.

If you can recommend something to people that then ultimately helps them, people will start to consider you a "go to" person for things, and those you refer business to also become likelier to refer business to you.

If you have a great product or service, help your customers help their people by making it easy for them to refer business to you.

A few things to keep in mind:

- There is an inherent risk for people in referring business to you. They are in a way lending their reputation. Don't give them a reason to feel there is risk involved. How can you minimise it?

- People do not refer business to boring businesses or those that are "just okay." They refer business to those that they think are great, businesses they love. You need to have a great product or service, but you also need to take into account the total experience—all the touchpoints with your brand. Great companies are not created by accident, and those that achieve greatness will not need to spend as much money and time on their marketing.

- Trust is key. This is something you simply have to earn by keeping your word, doing the right thing, managing your customers' expectations, and then exceeding them, rather than falling short. This is also something that needs to be built through each and every touchpoint with your brand and there are a lot of things discussed in this book that can help with building trust. For example, it is more likely than not that people will go online to check you out once they've heard of you. What will they find? Will it make them trust you?

- Just like you should have set up a system for your marketing in general, you should set up a system to get referrals. Find the best ways to encourage them and use those ways, rather than just hope and pray.

- When setting up a referral system, there are four main things you need to consider:
  - Who is going to refer business to you?
    - ➤ Generally, your customers and collaborators
    - ➤ Which ones?
    - ➤ How do you spot them?
    - ➤ Why do they recommend you?
    - ➤ What can you do to help them do more of it?
  - What do they need to know to be able to refer business to you?
    - ➤ You want them to know what kind of customers you want—so you don't have to keep turning the wrong kind of people away.

- ➤ How do you want them to introduce you and your offer?
- o What is the best way to get them to refer business to you and to remind them?
  - ➤ People may be more than willing to refer business to you, but we're all busy and things fall through the cracks. How can you ensure they follow through?
- o What are you going to do to follow up on that referral?

Like everything else in your marketing, referrals will work best when you are focused and organised in going about getting them.

Retargeting

Retargeting, also called remarketing, has come in strong in the past years, and it can be used on multiple online ad platforms, such as Google Ads, Facebook, YouTube, and more. Basically, when someone visits your website or performs some other action, such as watching your video, they are marked with a pixel (also called a cookie), allowing you to identify them, so you can advertise to them. If you've spent any time online, it is most likely that you have experienced being retargeted. For example, you have checked out an online store and for the next few days or weeks, you keep seeing ads from that store—even for exactly the stuff you were looking at. Sound familiar? If nothing pops to mind right now, take notice next time you are online and visit a website. Chances are, for the next few days, weeks, and even months, ads from that website seem to follow you around the world wide web.

Retargeting allows you to target only people you know are interested in what you have to offer, because they have already visited your website or interacted in some way with your content. Any tool that can help you sift out those not interested, so that you are not spending money and effort on talking to them in your marketing, is definitely worth checking out.

What's more, not only can you mark those that come to your website or have interacted with your content in general, you can identify exactly which page on your site they have been to, which video they have watched, etc., giving you an ability to target them even more specifically based on their interests. If they've checked out blue women's running shoes, you can target them with adverts only showing blue running shoes, or the same type of running shoe in other colours. Hey, that's what they were checking out, so why show them tennis racquets? ;)

The fact is that only a tiny percentage of the people who visit your website or interact with your content will buy or sign up, or whatever it is you want them to do when they come in contact with you. By continuing to remind them of the product or service they have already shown interest in, you can considerably increase those conversions.

Sales Promotions: Discounts and Offers

Discounts and offers of all sorts are a very well-known way to encourage sales. There are many variations of them, and you will find a list of some of them below, just to give you ideas.

It is important to realise that this is a very delicate marketing tool and, if used incorrectly can have a very negative effect on your brand, devaluing it, as well as negatively affecting profits in other ways. After all, if people are always seeing deals and discounts from you, why would they ever buy anything at full price?

You may, however, want to use them, for example if you want to increase sales during specific times, get people to buy sooner, give people a strong push to buy now, get rid of stock that is not selling well, get people to try things out, and for various other reasons.

You do need to make sure you don't always have deals running, because gradually you will teach people never to pay full price for your products and services.

How you use discounts and offers is also important. As a general rule of thumb, not changing the price on the ticket, but giving people more for their money, is better than lowering prices. This is simple human nature. If you see the actual number going down, you really don't like seeing it go up again. However, if the number stays the same, and you get a bit more bang for your buck for a certain amount of time, you don't feel as frustrated when you go back to getting what you usually get.

I'm sure you've seen this in action, particularly when it comes to fast moving consumer goods. Sometimes you get a bigger bottle of shampoo, and the promo says something like "20% more for the same price." Same price—more shampoo. Then when the bottle goes back to its regular size, you'll probably just keep buying it, all other things being equal. You just got a bonus for a while, which may have caused you to choose that brand above another and hence try it. You're okay when things go back to normal.

Bonus offers are also better for your image. If you think about it, this is well known in the cosmetics industry, where preserving the brand's image is paramount. For example, as I'm looking for examples of this, I find an ad for Clinique saying that if you buy for $28 or more, you get a free 7-piece gift with a value of $70, which includes miniature versions of makeup remover, moisturising lotion, eyeshadow, mascara, lipstick, and perfume. There is no discount. The products maintain their luxury image, but you are just getting a bit more. Generally speaking, adding value is better than discounting.

Also, provide a clear reason for the promotion. That way, people will accept that there is a promotion now, but this will change. It could be an introductory offer for a new product or service or an event-related offer (Valentine's Day, back to school, World Cup, or whatever). That will limit the offer to something specific, and people will be fully aware that once the promotion or event is over, prices will go back to normal.

In his book, *Marketing Plans*, Malcolm McDonald puts forward a great example to show the things you need to take into consideration when offering a discount. In his example, you have a product which sells at £10, with £2 from that being your profit margin. If you then offer a 10% discount, which puts the price at £9 and the profit margin at £1, this means your profit margin is now only 50 percent of what it was before, which in turn means you have to sell *twice* as much at that price to get the same profit.[19]

You have to think and do the math when you are discounting. You might decide that the loss in profit is a marketing cost you are willing to bear to get a product trial, reduce stock, or for whatever reason. Just make sure there is a valid reason.

Here is a list of some different types of promotions, just to give you ideas:

- Offers based on limited time or supply (until a certain date, "while stocks last").
- Event-based offers, such as around holidays, special events, and such.
- Coupons: Coupons are a good way to measure the results of your promotion. You can use them, for example, by putting the same advert in different media and see which ones give you the best returns. For this, you would need to identify the coupons from one media to the other with different codes and then you can see from which medium you get more coupons being handed in. Even better than having a discount coupon, have an added value coupon, as discussed above, to avoid negatively affecting your brand.

- Competitions and lucky draws.

- Follow-up offers, as discussed before. Offer your customer a deal on something related to what they just bought. They are still positive toward you and may well still be in a buying mood, and even more so if they feel like they are getting a special insider's deal. ;)

- Reader offers: Again, this is a tool which gives you a great chance to measure results. People will need to let you know where they got the deal, and you can thereby measure how effective that promo, medium, and ad are.

- 2 for 1, 3 for 2, etc. This is a great example of a promotion that adds value, rather than discounts. The price does not change, but for a limited time or while stocks last, people get more for their money.

- Bonus: As discussed before, adding value is better to maintain brand image than using other kinds of deals and discounts. The price stays the same, but the value is increased for a limited time.

- Getting x% extra for a limited time—remember that bigger shampoo bottle. ;)

- Introductory offer—people won't be expecting that *again.*

- Group discounts, where people get a deal if a certain number of people buy (the best known of these is probably Groupon in America).

- Gift vouchers. These can be given when people buy something else from you, and this is great for marketing partnerships. Give them a gift voucher for one of your partner's products or services.

Search Engine Marketing (SEM) aka Paid Search

See also: Google Ads, Pay-Per-Click Advertising, Keyword Analysis

Search engine marketing primarily refers to pay-per-click ads in search engine results. The best known would be the ads you get at the top, and to the right, of the results of your Google search.

TripAdvisor

If you are in the tourism and travel business, you need to be on TripAdvisor. It is as simple as that. This is where people go to look for accommodation, restaurants, activities, and even flights. Be there, and make sure you get as much out of your listing as possible.

On TripAdvisor, you can find free webinars about online marketing and how you can increase your bookings, and they teach you how to use their free tools. They also have recordings of previous webinars on lots of things that you may find useful. Make use of them.

TripAdvisor is the first stop in travel planning for a lot of people, so it is absolutely a tool for **awareness**. A good profile with good photos, information, and reviews can gain **interest** and build **like**ability and **trust**.

Reviews can get people through the **trial** part of the marketing process, and **sales** can take place on the site (conversion). And TripAdvisor is by its very nature a **referral** tool.

Video

Videos can be a great marketing tool, and they just become easier and easier to use. They are popular on social media and can often communicate things much better than text and still images—some sources claim that video is 300 percent more effective than text![20]

Video can be used in a variety of ways. Some businesses might just have one good promo video done and use it wherever appropriate. Others have a video series professionally done, and yet others may do regular videos inhouse. Video blogs or vlogs are very popular and so-called explainer videos are, as well, explaining things that your prospective customers need to know, in a simple visual way. Slide videos are quick and simple but catch the eye more than still images, and there are a now a lot of online services allowing you to make them yourself for a low price. The possibilities are endless. You simply have to think about whether and then how videos can work for you.

A good online video that goes viral can create **awareness** and **interest**, as people are not really likely to be sharing it unless it's interesting ;) (lead generation). By optimising for search, on places such as YouTube and Facebook, through keywords and other methods, getting videos found online can be a great awareness tool, as well. You can definitely use videos to build **like**ability and **trust**, depending on the content and quality of the video (lead nurturing).

Videos are a great way to give people a "taste" of what you have to offer, not in the least for things like services, where it can be hard to give people a good idea of what they are getting beforehand (**trial**). A good video can even convey experience quite strongly, really giving people a feel for what they will be getting.

With the right kind of content and use, you can use video to encourage **repeat sales** and help **referrals**.

A Few More Ideas

Affiliate Marketing

Affiliate marketing is about partnering with others who have an audience that is a good fit for you to sell your product or service, and they will take a commission (generally 30 to 50 percent). Affiliate marketing is most common in online business, but it can be used in other situations. Selling through an affiliate network, such as Rakuten, ShareaSale or Clickbank, can help get your product or service in front of the right audience and endorsed by someone that already has a relationship with them and they **know, like, and trust**. Hence, this makes them more willing to buy. Affiliate marketing is, therefore, by its very nature a **referral** tool.

Amazon

Do you have a product that would fit on Amazon? If so, that's just where you may want to be. You can sell your products through Amazon and even have them take care of all the fulfilment and customer service.

Amazon is essentially just one huge search engine for products, so it makes sense to feature yours where people actually come to search for them and buy. It's a bit like having a shop in a mall, rather than in suburbia. ;)

Depending on where you are in the world, you want to choose the right Amazon Seller Central to register with. They have good information about how the whole thing works, so if you think this may be something for you, go check it out. ;)

Apps

Apps are becoming more and more popular and can be used in marketing in various ways. However, this is neither a cheap nor simple marketing method, so you need to think about this carefully and do your research before going down that route.

A common mistake businesses make is to have an app made when a good mobile responsive website could have done the same thing. Apps are both more expensive to make and maintain than websites, but there is also the challenge of actually getting people to download your app and use it. If you do get them to do that, though, you are a constant reminder on their phone.

Apps are an option you may want to look into, but before you jump into creating one, make sure you do your research and consider things carefully.

Attend Networking Events

Remember that business network we talked about before? ;)

If there are events where you know the people you want to meet and get to know will be, go to them!

You will also find events that are directly set up for networking. There are a lot of variations, but one of the most fun ways I've heard of is events that are set up in the same way as speed dating events, except their purpose is to establish business connections.

Make sure you make use of every opportunity like this to build your network. Network building can only be good for your business ;)

Associations, Clubs, and Networks

Yet again, it's all about building that network. Joining relevant associations or networks is a great way to connect with people. These could be general networks like Rotary, Chambers of Commerce, Toastmasters, or industry specific networks applicable to your business. These could be associations where you are a professional involved on behalf of your company or more personal ones that still allow you to build contacts and get some exposure for your business. There are a wealth of great networks and associations all over the place. Find the right ones for you, join and see what you can get out of them.

Birthday Greetings

Most people love it when someone remembers their birthday and sending a birthday greeting is a simple way to stay in touch and evoke positive feelings.

How you do this will depend on what is right for you. If you are a consultant with only a handful of big and high-ticket clients, this may be in the form of sending a fancy bottle of red wine or whiskey or a box of chocolates with a card.

If you are in retail with lots of small customers, this can simply be a part of your email marketing. Invite them to give information about their birthdate when they sign up for your email list, and then use autoresponders to let your email system send those greetings out automatically. Some retailers also give people a discount on their birthday or even a little present to be picked up the next time they are in store or order online—who says no to a birthday present? ;)

However you choose to do this, everyone loves a little "Happy Birthday!"

Brochure / Leaflet / Flyer

Brochures, leaflets, and flyers are well established marketing tools that have been used for ages. If you think they may be useful for you, by all means use them. I do want to ask you, however, to think long and hard about this and not to use them unless you really think they are necessary and best for you.

You can have a wealth of information available online, whenever and wherever, and it is easy to update it there. Brochures and leaflets, on the other hand, cost a lot of money to design, print, and distribute, and once you have, there is no updating. They are also environmentally unfriendly, and, unfortunately, far too many of them are thrown in the bin before they ever get read.

If you decide to use brochures or leaflets, make sure you have a good reason to and make sure they have great value, preferably enough to make people keep them, rather than throw them in the next bin. Think Ikea—theirs is probably one of the few brochures that can be justified, as their prices are valid for a year from publication, and we know that many people keep them safe and refer to them again and again and again. Like me, you might also have friends who look forward to it arriving through their letterbox and have a cosy night on the sofa drinking red wine and browsing the Ikea catalogue!

Cause Marketing

Giving is good, and I encourage you to support a good cause. Doing so is also just good business—and good karma. ;) Various research shows that social responsibility and businesses supporting good causes matters more and more to customers, especially younger generations who prefer to do business with those who care.

Is there a cause which aligns particularly well with your business, product, or service? Something that you can make your own, help a good cause, and build your image in a positive way whilst doing it?

A number of my clients have done these kinds of things—for example, sponsoring children in school, supporting nature preservation, getting involved in Movember, and more. Global brands have been built with good causes at their core, such as Toms shoes, which gives shoes, sight, water, safe birth, and bullying prevention services in over 70 countries around the world (toms.com/what-we-give), and Body Shop, which built their brand by supporting the fight against animal cruelty in the cosmetics industry.

Do your bit for society and good causes. Let the world know about it—but make sure that you walk the talk. Don't ever just put this on for show. You will soon be found out, and it will do more harm than good. If you can do good by using your product or service in some way, even better.

Classified Ads

There are still niches out there for which classified ads work like a charm. They are an affordable option, and the price may enable you to advertise regularly and do some testing to see what works best for you.

You don't need to have a classified ad in each edition of your chosen publication, but it is good. Remember: consistency and repetition. ;) As with any other media usage, you need to make sure you are advertising in the right publication for you, that your target group is there, and you need to figure out how you are going to measure the results of your efforts.

Are you going to include a coupon code for a discount or bonus to measure the results? Are you simply going to ask your customers where they found out about you or do some other form of market research?

Make sure you consider your brand and the fact that just by using classified ads you are affecting your brand image. Who else advertises there? The company you keep in the classifieds can influence the way you are perceived.

Also consider that classifieds are not the best tool for *generally* building awareness, as they are usually not read by people unless they are looking for something specifically in that ad category.

Client Meetings

Client meetings may seem like an obvious marketing activity, but how many of us make sure we manage them systematically and effectively?

If you have the sort of business where client meetings are appropriate (obviously, if you have thousands of customers for a low-priced offering, it won't be), make sure you meet your clients regularly to maintain your relationship. This could be for lunch or a cup of coffee or invite them for a visit or drop by their place. Determining the right thing for you will depend on your industry and business.

A consultant with only a handful of big clients could have lunch with them regularly. If you sell things through retailers, you may want to meet up with those retailers, as they are your clients. These are the shop owners that buy your things to resell to the end user; make sure to maintain a good relationship with them.

Meeting your clients can greatly impact who they do business with and which suppliers they prioritise in those all-important shop shelves (whether brick-and-mortar or online). We do business with people, and we build relationships with people. Don't ever forget the human touch. ;)

Competitions and Prize Draws

Competitions and prize draws can be a way to get to people to check out your products and services. There are various ways to do this. An oldie, but goodie, is simply to have people answer questions whose answers they could find on your website, thereby getting people to go quite thoroughly through your online content. With the advent of social media, various online competitions and prize draws have popped up, as well.

There are a lot of things to consider when running competitions and prize draws, including rules and regulations that need to be adhered to. These, of course, vary between types of competitions and prize draws and the platforms you use to conduct them. They may also vary by country. If this is something you want to use in your marketing, make sure you get all the info you need and, where relevant, seek expert advice on how to do them.

You also need to make sure you are attracting your target audience. Facebook games with iPad prizes were all the rage at one point, but who doesn't want an iPad? The majority of those entering probably didn't have any interest in the product or service being marketed at all, so it was pointless to attract them. When it comes to Facebook and endless similar games, it is also worth noting that having loads of likes on your page is useless if there are not real and engaged people behind those likes. That could result in a page with very low engagement, hence, even lower visibility than Facebook provides for free already (which is practically non-existent, really).

Customer Relationship Management Software (CRM)

As stated numerous times before, your network is one of your most powerful marketing tools. You must manage it effectively. The simplest way to do this is with your contacts book. I always recommend that it is at least electronic and cloud based. Those little black books can get lost, stolen, burnt ... ;)

It is also simple and even free in some cases to use Customer Relationship Management (CRM) software. With CRM, you can record every aspect of your communications with your contacts, get reminders when you should get in touch again, when to call, when to email. Well used CRMs also ensure that no matter who people talk to within your business, your staff all know what is going on and have the necessary information and story of the relationship. Do keep in mind that the system won't do all this on its own—it is merely a tool, so proper staff onboarding and processes to ensure the most effective use of the system are necessary.

Do a Google search for CRM software and you will find lots of information about them, as well as a lot of good options from which to choose.

Direct Mail

Direct Mail (DM) is an oldie but a goodie. Strictly speaking, DM is not classed as DM unless you can have measurable responses, such as how many people called the telephone number promoted or how many people used the coupon included. Today the term DM is often used for a much wider range of marketing tools, basically any kind of stuff that goes directly to people's homes or offices.

Doing a blanket mailing to certain geographical areas is usually more affordable than direct mail targeted at a specific person by name (Targeted Direct Mail or TDM). However, with good targeting, you may actually get a better return on investment with TDM because you are not wasting anything on people who aren't right for the offer. Depending on your business, it may be much more effective to send TDM to a small group of people at a time, and then follow up with them, than just throwing DMs all over the place, including at people who are in no way suited for your product or services.

Whether you use general or targeted DM, there are a few things I want to mention. This is not an exhaustive list of things to consider when using DM, just a few things I think are particularly important:

Think of your DM as content marketing, rather than advertising. What would people like to get from you? What can you send them that would actually make them happy to get your DM, rather than frustrated, making them throw it straight in the bin like we do with so much junk mail?

Try to find a way to make your DM good enough in content and / or design that people actually want to keep it. If they pin it on their board or put it on the fridge, it will be more effective and provide a constant reminder of your brand. This may make it a bit more expensive to produce, but it should also make it work much, much harder for you.

Before you use printed DM, consider the environment. Can you reach people through simpler, more affordable, and more environmentally friendly ways? If so, please do. ;)

eBay

Just like Amazon, eBay is an online shopping mall and as such attracts people looking for all sorts of things. This may, therefore, be the right place for you. If you have a product that is a good fit for eBay, you should definitely look into being there.

You want to be where your potential customers are. Being in online stores such as Amazon, eBay, or others that attract your target audience is like being at the mall where people come, whereas having your own standalone online store is a bit like having a shop in the middle of nowhere and having to really, really pull people *to you.*

Check out eBay's help pages for detailed information on how to go about selling through eBay.

Electronic Newsletter

Whether we call it email marketing or sending an electronic newsletter is just a question of how we want to define things and how we want to present them. How does the email look? What does it contain? How often is it sent?

Newsletters are clearly more formal in their layout and design than a lot of other types of email marketing. They include news and should be sent regularly but are likely to be sent less frequently than other types of email marketing and may even have a publication number.

It's all a question of how you approach things and how you present them. What's right for your brand? Formal businesses are likelier to have newsletters, but more informal ones simply have emails. You need to determine what is right for you.

Etsy

Etsy is an online sales site where you can set up your own shop if you are selling handmade things, vintage items, and supplies for arts and crafts. If you sell any of these, you should definitely check it out, for the same reasons as you may want to look into selling through Amazon or eBay if you have appropriate products for those.

Setting up an Etsy store is easy, and there is no fixed cost. At the time of this writing, you pay a little something for listing your product and then a set fee and a percentage of your sales. This can be an extremely simple and convenient way to set up an online store in a short amount of time and be where a lot of people are looking. It can also be a good way to get your first online store going, before embarking on a larger endeavour of your own online shop with all the work that can entail—including the work involved in getting people to visit it.

Etsy will lead you through setting up your shop and offers a lot of good stuff about marketing on its site, including discussion groups.

Free Consultation

A variation on the well-known tactic of giving out free product samples and service trials is a free consultation. Whether you sell consultation services and offer something like a 30-minute free consultation at the start, or you use the free consultation to then sell a product or other service packages, this can be great for awareness, likeability, and letting people get to know you.

Make sure this is realistic for you to manage. Ensure that it doesn't take too much time from paid consultations and other revenue-generating tasks in your business. Also, keep in mind that this is not very scalable, i.e., you cannot offer it to very many people at a time, so the consultations really need to work for you and the cost of them needs to be worth the business it can generate.

You can also give free consultation through events in your industry, if applicable. For example, I often provide free consultation at various innovation and entrepreneurship events, such as Startup Weekend and UnConference, and at various business accelerator programs. This creates awareness of me but also gives people a chance to meet me and see what I have to offer. (I do also just love to get back to the grassroots of business and do my bit to help build new businesses. :))

Free Courses

Just like free trials, demonstrations, or consultations, free courses can be a good way to get the word out and gain attention. People do tend to like you if you give them something like this that is of interest and value to them, and if the course is good, this will build trust and give people the chance to try what you have to offer.

You would, of course, not give a big course involving a lot of time and work, but it may be worth your while to give even a 1-2 hour course if it has enough participants and you use the course to upsell further courses, consultation, products, or services.

These courses can be in person or online (webinar format). Consider having a special offer for those who attend the free course, making it even more worthwhile to attend. Note, you have to promote the free course, so this is mainly a lead capture and nurture tool, although it can also have lead conversion tactics built in.

Consider all these suggestions of free things (courses, consultation, and trials and demonstrations discussed below) in context with what we have covered already about content marketing and collaborative marketing.

Free Demonstration

Following on from free trials and free courses, offering a free demonstration of your product or service can be a good way to get business. This could be exactly what is needed to get people through the trial part of the process and get those interested to convert into customers.

The best way to do this depends on your business. Do you have something that can pull the crowds in to see you, or should you be where they are, whether that is out and about or even in their homes?

Home demonstrations are well known for businesses like Tupperware, SaladMaster, and Rainbow. In B2B settings, demos are very much used in software sales. Is this something that could work in your business?

Free demonstrations can work to raise awareness and interest, if taking place somewhere people are already, such as at the mall or an exhibition, and can nurture a lead and get them through the trial phase of the marketing process.

Free Trial

Does your product or service lend itself well to offering a free trial? Whether you offer a free trial on a general basis or just do it occasionally for promotional purposes, this could be something to consider for your marketing.

A free trial is often exactly what is needed to get the word out and gain interest (awareness and interest). People also tend to like those that give them free stuff, and this gives people a chance to get to know your business, product, or service. Trying things builds trust, and it gets people through the trial part of the marketing process.

Make sure the trial is worth something to the potential customers, whilst still making sure it is not too expensive or time consuming for you. Remember to be sure you are reaching the right target group(s) and that the trial is worth it for you—this should make more business than it costs you.

Free trials are commonly used for services, both online and offline.

Get Customers Involved in Product Trials and Development

By getting customers involved in trying out products or services in development, and hence involvement in the development, you could build buzz before getting it to the market. Also, getting customers' input in the development process is generally a good thing. ;)

Doing this could mean that the competition finds out what you are up to before you are prepared for that to happen, so that is a risk to be aware of (although non-disclosure agreements and other legal precautions can be used to protect from that). Of course, there is a lot more to this and many things to consider, but I'm just throwing this out here as an idea for you to be aware of. ;)

Gifts

Gifts can be a good marketing tool if used right.

Do you have a good, big, important, and loyal client? Give them a present for the holidays (Christmas, Hanukkah, or whatever holiday is appropriate), on their birthday, or just for fun.

Is there someone you really want to build a relationship with? Give them a gift. An important business connection? Make them happy with a little something.

Even if you have many smaller clients, you may be able to give them a little something just to show them that you appreciate them. This could even be in electronic format, such as an eBook or a video exclusively for your customers.

It goes without saying that you need to make sensible choices both with regard to what you give and how much it costs, but it's a great reminder and a way to show your customers you care (ongoing lead management).

Gift Certificates

Do you offer gift certificates? If not, you might be leaving money on the table.

Most B2C businesses can sell more by offering gift cards. This is a simple and affordable marketing tool. All it takes is paper and some ink—and it can be electronic. ;)

Gift certificates give those who are undecided the chance to still give someone a product or service from your business. Who doesn't know the feeling of holidays or birthdays looming and having to find the perfect gift for someone who has everything? Well, your gift card could be just the solution they are looking for!

Gift cards for services, activities, or experiences can be the perfect gift to give for those that don't want to add to the stuff in the world. There are also always quite a few gift cards that never even get used (I've heard figures up to 60 percent), which basically means that you are just given money.

Make sure you check the rules and regulations surrounding gift certificates in your country and adhere to them.

Giving Prizes

Most people running a business have been asked to donate things for this and that reason and to support this and that cause. There are classics, like giving awards for lucky draws at a club event, something to help local sports associations, something for the local bazaar, etc. Do you sell cosmetics? You may want to give awards for a female golf tournament or some kind of women's night. Do you sell beer? Give beer or a good discount on your product for that guys' night.

This can be great for visibility and goodwill, and I will never tell you not to support a good cause or your local community. However, I do want to encourage you to think about how you can get more marketing wise out of the support. If you are doing things, why shouldn't you make sure that you get the goodwill and awareness?

Make sure the gift looks awesome, is beautifully presented, and clearly branded. I can't tell you how often I have looked at a table full of prize draw gifts given by a number of local businesses and not had any idea what is what or who gave them because they simply didn't think to make sure they could be identified!

Group Buying Services

Group buying services, or deal-of-the-day services, are services that broker a deal between a business, prepared to offer a particular deal for their products or services, providing they reach a certain minimum of buyers and people looking for those sorts of deals. The one that put this business model on the mark is probably Groupon in America.

Group buying services can be used for marketing purposes, but you need to be careful how you use them. I know of examples where people have seen great results, but I also know of examples where this has been nothing but trouble.

Group buying services can be a good way to gain awareness of your offer and get people to try your business, which may then lead to further business. However, you should keep in mind that those who use these kinds of services a lot are the kind of people that are always looking for a deal. They are looking for offers and discounts and chasing the best price, so this may not be the best place to find long-term, loyal, and high-value customers.

You also have to make sure you can cater to the amount of business you may get through these kinds of services. This applies in particular if you are selling services, as opposed to products (although I've seen some product businesses fall really flat with this, as well). If you sell services at a huge discount to be able to offer a deal at a site like this, how much can you sell before it negatively affects your business? The site will take a big chunk of the money, don't forget that.

Group buying services are an option, but one you need to research and consider carefully before using.

Guarantee

Giving your customers some sort of guarantee, such as a full refund within a certain amount of days if they are not happy, or a seven-year warrant like Hyundai, will considerably minimise the perceived risk of buying and help the trial part of the marketing process.

You should, of course, be selling good products and services, so guaranteeing them is not something you should be afraid of.

If you do offer something like this, make sure people know about it when they are making their decision. This could be exactly the thing needed to clinch the deal. ;)

Guides and Instructions

Any kinds of guides or instructions are very popular in content marketing. They are also a great way to get your current customers to visit your website again and again, giving you the chance to introduce them to other products and services they may be interested in.

Save yourself the cost of printing guides or instructions for your products and services and instead direct people to your website, where you can also continually update them, as well as providing great opportunities in how you present the content, such as using video or interactive web content.

Have a Good Party!

During my MBA studies, I did a course on team building. I remember the professor, a PhD in workplace psychology, saying that the simplest way to get a group working together was to take them to the pub together. (Needless to say, I did my studies in London, England, the land of the pubs. ;))

Whilst I do not want to encourage excessive alcohol consumption, it is a fact that partying together can work miracles for business relationships. It always comes down to the fact that people do business with people, and people connect when having a good time.

Many businesses do this on a regular basis. I know of businesses that have big annual parties where they invite their clients and business partners to a good old knees-up without any shoptalk, just have fun and get to know each other better. This improves personal relationships, which improves business relationships.

Is this something you could do in your business?

Holiday Greetings

Holiday greetings are even simpler to do than birthday greetings. Each holiday only tends to be once a year ;) ... so you can send a blanket greeting to everyone! :) As with birthday greetings, what is appropriate depends on your business. Is it a simple email or social media message, a card, or a full on present?

Make sure you take good care of your list of customers, marketing partners, and your business network so you don't have to panic just before the holiday and pull all the details together at the last minute. Even retailers have some contacts that should get a more personal greeting than others. A general customer on the email list might only get a simple email, something on social media or in an ad, but you may want to send a more personal greeting to your suppliers and business partners. ;)

Influencer Marketing

Influencer marketing has been rising in the past years, particularly with the rise of Internet celebrities from platforms such as YouTube and Instagram, as well as bloggers. With audiences that can range up to tens of millions, these influencers can have a lot of sway, and one endorsement from the right influencer can make a huge difference to your sales. Therefore, getting your product in the hands of an influencer, such as a celebrity, or letting it be known that they have used your services, can be great in marketing.

However, this is easier said than done, as influencers get tons of requests for endorsements and are inundated with gifts from businesses wanting to use them to get their stuff in front of people. You may be able to get smaller influencers to endorse your product by simply giving it to them, particularly smaller local ones. However, generally you have to pay for the endorsement, the way you would with an advert.

In some industries, opinion leaders need not be celebrities or people who make their living off endorsements. In that case, you may not have to pay for endorsements, but may need to find other ways to get their support. Who affects people's opinion in your industry? Who are the trendsetters, movers, and shakers? Who is leading the discussion? Can you establish contact and get them to endorse your product or service in some way?

Today, you can find a lot of influencer marketing agencies, whose sole purpose is to connect influencers with brands. A strong network can also be useful, particularly when getting in touch with smaller celebrities. If you know them, or know someone who knows them, you are already a few steps ahead of all the others that do not have any connection.

Make sure the influencer you are going to work with is in alignment with your brand, has the same values, and appeals to your target audience. Also, make sure they are not for sale to just anyone who offers enough money. If they promote you this week and your competitor next week, the endorsement has no credibility. And don't think that influencer endorsement is a silver bullet. It may work like a charm, but it also may not do everything you expect it to do. You also need to do all the "normal" marketing stuff ;).

If you can connect your product or service to an influencer that appeals to your target audience, that can work like a referral. Whether by endorsement, as discussed before, or indirectly by bringing attention to the fact that they have used the product or service, this can help. Examples are when restaurants publicise that someone has dined at their establishment (after the fact, is prudent ;)) or when they are seen in the media wearing your clothes.

A final and very important note: there are huge legal and ethical implications to using influencer marketing. A detailed discussion is outside the scope of this book but make sure you adhere to all applicable rules and regulations and always ensure the influencer discloses that this is a paid promotion.

Invite People to Visit

Do you have a business which could accommodate inviting groups to visit, look at and experience your business? Could you tell them about something fun, interesting, or useful? Or are you just fun and exciting in and of yourself? Or do you give the best parties?

Inviting people to visit can be good for your marketing. This introduces people to your business and gives people a chance to get to know you. Make sure you have some way of capturing those leads coming into your business. One way would be to get them to sign up to your email list.

A client of mine who is a designer hosts an open workshop on various occasions, such as in the run up to the holidays. People drop by, have a cup of mulled wine, browse her designs, and pick up a couple of Christmas presents. It's a lovely and relaxed way to shop and really builds the relationship with her customers.

Also embracing this way of marketing are smaller alcohol producers, such as microbreweries, wine makers, and whiskey distilleries, with tastings, tours of the facilities and such.

Think about what kinds of groups would be good for you to invite for a visit and on what occasions? These could be staff groups, clubs or associations, students, groups of friends, etc. This may not be for every business, but I've had clients who have seen great results by doing this.

Inviting the Media for a Visit

Staying with the previous idea of inviting prospective customers to visit you, how about inviting the media? You can invite them for a tour of the company, to experience the service, try your product, or whatever else is relevant for you. Keep in mind, though, that media people are constantly being offered all sorts of things to try to get them to give media coverage, so you need to offer something extremely interesting for them to bother coming. And once you've got them there, the experience needs to be awesome because a bad experience could do a lot more harm than good. ;)

Is this something you could do?

Marketing While You Wait

Do you have a waiting area, or does your target audience often use waiting areas somewhere else? Marketing while people wait can be quite effective, not just by using adverts such as posters, stands and such, which you can of course do, but also through content marketing. You can use this at your premises or with a marketing partner that shares your target group.

If you sell hair products, a magazine or a screen showing a video with advice about taking care of your hair or how to achieve some great hairstyles might be just the thing to have at hair salons while people wait to be served.

If you sell products that help prevent sports injuries, this might be something you want to promote at the physio clinic or the gym.

Advice on how to do breast examinations for cancer is exactly the kind of thing to have at the OBGYN's waiting area.

What could you do?

Merchandising

Merchandising is a marketing classic. Who hasn't got at least one branded pen, mug, or writing pad? ;)

Merchandising can be a great way to give your customers something and get constant visibility in exchange. By giving them something useful and of value to them, you are also helping your likeability factor. :)

However, for a small business, merchandising can get expensive, so you need to think about this carefully. Sometimes you will also find it is better to buy something more expensive that people will actually like and keep, rather than skimp and give some junk that people get rid of straight away—and won't do your brand image or the environment any good, either. That totally defeats the objective. And then sometimes you may think you are buying something good, but it turns out to be junk (pens, anyone?), so do your research before you buy.

There is no lack of businesses that offer promotional merchandise, so you won't have any problem finding one, if not locally, then online. Finding the *right thing* and the *right business* to do business with may be a bit trickier, however, so do your groundwork. ;)

Online Groups

Having a closed online group can be a great marketing tool. It can be open to anyone, giving you a chance to nurture leads once they're in there and customer groups (VIP, "insiders only") can be a great way to stay in touch with your customers (ongoing lead management). This is a place for discussions, asking questions, getting answers and for your business to contribute to the conversation and exchange advice and information—you need to be active in there, of course. Really, online groups are pure content marketing, which gives you the opportunity to build your relationships and be the "go to" resource.

Getting a group like this going and keeping up the activity level can be a bit of work, but it can be well worth it. This is not just you giving, as with most content marketing, but participants are also giving to each other through discussions, answers, and feedback. Online customer groups can also increase the likelihood of repeat business and referrals.

Online groups can be set up on various platforms, and you have to choose the one that best fits your audience and business. You can use tools such as Google Groups, LinkedIn Groups, or Facebook groups (probably the most popular option), and you can also have your own online forum. You may find it is easier to be where your customers are already, as they are likelier to drop in from there. That's why Facebook is such a popular place for groups, because people are already hanging out on Facebook. It can be quite hard to drag people to something like your own forums, for example.

A few ideas and examples of how you might use online groups:

Do you offer financial consulting or bookkeeping? Set up an open group where you give tips and advice and another one for your clients where you can give deeper and more detailed tips and advice, remind them of important dates and such. Go in regularly and answer questions, share useful information, etc.

Are you a personal fitness trainer? Have a group where you can share recipes, exercises, and encourage people to share their results. Answer questions regularly, throw in some good advice or just something encouraging and motivating, a lively tune on a Friday or whatever else you think will work. Always remember to give your customer group more value than the open group – it's yet another reason for people to become a customer.

Are you in tourism and get a lot of foreign tourists? Have an "insiders" group on Facebook with customers and encourage them to share pictures, stories, and advice. Add people to the group as soon as they book with you, so they can benefit from the information and activity in there and get them even more excited about visiting you. Feature useful information. Use photo albums and files to feature information about things like what people can do in your area, a map, information about hiking routes, opening hours, etc. Be their information centre and the place where they can get information and answers to their questions.

What could you do with an online group?

Open Day / Open House

Is your business suited to having an open day or open house when people come and learn more about your business? This can be a great way to introduce services that may be hard to explain in other ways (get that demonstration in) or get people to understand, and to meet people and let them get to know your business.

Hosting an open house can be a challenge, and you need to make sure that you feature things that will attract your target audience. Some refreshments, entertainment, interesting talks, or demonstrations are just some of the things that may attract interest.

Promoting the event is in itself another marketing task, but if you have something interesting to show people, you should consider this option. Also, if there is something else going on in your area that this can be linked to, such as town festivals or holidays, this can be great as people may already be out and about and interested in dropping by.

Podcast

A podcast is really your own online radio show, except people can download the episodes and listen to them at their convenience. They have been having quite the revival in the past few years and only seem to be becoming a more and more popular way of consuming content. There are a number of great things about podcasts, such as:

- People can consume them at their own convenience, and they can do it while they are doing something else (driving, at the gym, cleaning...), as opposed to reading blogs or watching videos which takes up all of their attention, so they have less free time available to consume them.

- People tend to consume longer content through podcasts than other mediums because they can consume it while doing other things. That means longer time with you. ;)

- People can "binge listen" to your podcast *when they* want to. And in this day and age of binge consumption of media, that is a very good thing.

- Audio connects in a way that blogging cannot. They are actually hearing your voice, as opposed to just reading your words, creating a much more intimate connection.

- For those who aren't comfortable writing, and those who don't want to be on camera, audio can be a very comfortable medium. Just hit the record button and start talking. ;)

Podcasting is becoming more and more popular as a marketing tool, and you will find that many of the best-known online marketing gurus have their own podcasts, with good results. Trust me, people like Ryan Deiss, Sonia Simone, Tim Ferriss, Amy Porterfield, and many more would not be spending their time podcasting unless it was working for them.

Whether podcasting is right for you will, as always, depend on your target audience, and, of course, whether it is something you feel comfortable with, but it might be worth considering. If you have a product or service that lends itself to creating audio content around it, this might be just what the marketing doctor ordered.

Podcasting is pure content marketing, with the ability to create awareness (with the proper use of distribution channels), interest, and a very strong ability to build the like and trust factor. According to various sources, podcast listeners are buying products and services after hearing about them on a podcast.

Post Cards / Referral Cards

You can have postcards / referral cards printed and have them in appropriate places for people to see and take, and you can give a bunch to people who are able to refer business to you. This is similar to using flyers and in some ways similar to having general business cards for your business (see above).

Make sure it looks good, is on brand, has all the necessary information, and even has an incentive to get in touch, such as a discount or bonus. In that way, you can also measure how effective they are through the ones that make their way back to you. ;)

Presentations or Promotional Events

This is a bit like having a demonstration, free course, and such, as discussed previously, except here we are simply talking about a presentation or demonstration of your product or service.

You can have these events yourself, which means you need to promote the event itself or get partners to promote it (see marketing partnerships above). Bringing the presentation or demonstration to people where they are, such as at clubs and associations, can also be a great way to reach your audience.

QR Codes

QR codes (quick response codes) are a type of barcode which can have more information than a typical barcode. People can scan the code with their smartphone and be led to a website, text, app or a variety of other things. These can be used in various ways, but there is still quite a bit of discussion as to how well this works marketing wise.

Don't get carried away with QR codes. Sometimes it's just simpler to give people the URL to type in than get them to open an app, scan, and be taken in that way. ;)

Reprints and Enlargements

If you get a great piece of coverage in the media, and have an office, shop, waiting room, or another place to which your customers come, you might want to have that piece of coverage printed in good quality and show it off to get even more mileage out of it.

This, of course, applies particularly if you have got some really good coverage in top notch media. If, for example, you get your beauty product featured in *Vogue*, that will impress people who see it.

This can be tricky, because things can easily get shabby if you hang these kinds of things all over the place, but if you do it in a tasteful way, this can help get you even more attention, likeability, and trust. ;)

Oh, and you should, of course, also have featured that media coverage on your website and social media. ;)

Samples

If you have a product that lends itself to samples, that is always a useful thing. Whether you just distribute them everywhere your target audience can be found, or they are featured in a good spot with a call to action for people to grab them, they can increase visibility and give people the opportunity to try before buying.

Samples can build awareness and interest, if they are presented in front of the right audience, and when people try the product this way, it can build like, trust, and is, of course, a trial. :)

SMS Marketing

I am not a fan of text message marketing, as I find it very intrusive, but that's a personal thing and this is an option. It is important to remember, as with email marketing, that people need to give their approval for receiving marketing messages, and they must also have a clear option of unsubscribing, such as by replying with the word "STOP" or in another clear and simple way. Use at your own discretion, but make sure you adhere to all applicable rules and regulations.

Stunts and Guerrilla Marketing

Marketing or PR stunts are well known and have long been used to get attention. If your brand lends itself to this kind of thing and you or your team are creative and inventive enough, this can be both fun and very effective. It can even get you into the media and / or spread virally online.

There are no limits to what you can do with things like this—only your imagination. I've seen some fantastic examples, such as putting chalk ads and pictures on sidewalks, giant objects as outdoor advertising, and projects that could just as well be art installations. Flash mobs are another fun stunt. Can you do something fun and a bit crazy to bring attention to your brand? :)

In the reader resources at thoranna.is/mcureader, you can find a link to a collection of some great marketing stunts.

These kinds of stunts are also often called guerrilla marketing, which is why I included that in this heading. However, the true definition of guerrilla marketing, à la the godfather of guerrilla marketing, Jay Conrad Levinson, is really not about these crazy kinds of stunts but simply about really good and professional marketing. Or as he says in his book, *Guerrilla Marketing Remix*, *"Guerrilla marketing embraces 360 degrees of communication, reaching target audiences in as many ways as are affordable and possible. Your task as a guerrilla is to be aware of all the marketing weapons available to you, to experiment with many of them, and then to identify the combination of weapons that provides the highest profit to you."*[21]

Swag Bags

A swag bag is basically a bag of products given to guests at an event. Some of us have only ever heard about this being done in Hollywood and the music business, but a lot of other events have swag bags for their guests.

If your target group attends the sort of events that have swag bags, getting your product in there can be a great thing. It gets you awareness and gives people a chance to try your stuff.

You may be able to get into smaller and local events just by giving your products or services, but if you want to get into the bags at some of the larger events, you may have to pay to get in there. Make sure that the event is in alignment with your brand. A great event can be fantastic for your brand image, but a bad one can also do a lot of harm.

Trade Shows

If your industry has them, trade shows could be a powerful marketing tool for you. They are, however, also expensive if you want to set up a booth and really do them properly. I would suggest starting by doing research into which shows are relevant to you. Which are the biggest? Which seem to have most of the people you want to reach? Are you looking for resellers, or do you want to sell straight to consumers? This will affect how you use trade shows in your marketing.

There are many things to consider. The first time around, going to the show as a guest can be a good start. Bring plenty of business cards and don't be stingy with them. If you can easily grab a few products or have good marketing materials for products or services that you can't bring with you, bring what you can. You never know when good opportunities may present themselves.

When you decide to have a larger presence at the show, consider sharing one with another business that shares your target audience as a way to reduce the cost, and benefit from any synergies in pulling in guests (obviously not a competitor ;)). This can be a way to have a presence without emptying the piggy bank.

Before taking part, I recommend talking to someone with experience in trade shows—even better if it is someone who knows the particular show you are considering attending. This could save you a lot of time, work, and headache. Remember that network you are building—do you know anyone with knowledge in this area? ;)

Translations and Publishing

By translating and publishing quality content in your area of expertise, you may be able to show that you are an expert in your field and have your finger on the pulse. You could also make some money from the sales of those publications. This could be a book, magazine articles, or other types of content. It is an option for some to consider.

Win an Award and Use It in Your Marketing

Are there any awards in your area of business? Look into it and see what needs to be done to be considered for them.

Many think that one day someone will just nominate them for an award which they may then get. The fact is, though, in most cases you simply have to apply yourself! So why not do that?

Winning an award can be great for your marketing if you make the most of it. This really helps the trust and trial part of the marketing process. The next time you see that some business, product, or service has received an award (even an award you have never heard about), note your reaction. Even if you've never heard of the award, you will automatically think higher of that business, product, or service.

Write a Book

Writing a book can be a fantastic way to make your mark as an expert in your industry and get awareness and credibility. This can also open up a lot of opportunities, such as getting you into media, doing public speaking, etc. You didn't think I wrote the *Marketing Untangled* Series only to share my wisdom with you, did you? ;) The first books in the series have already helped open doors for me, such as speaking gigs and getting featured in media.

Writing a book and publishing it is not actually as hard as you may think, particularly in this day and age of eBooks, Amazon, and self-publishing.

Writing Columns or Articles

If you are a good writer, you may want to consider writing for media. Take a look at the media that is relevant for your brand and you would like to write for. Then systematically go about building relationships with the appropriate people there with a view to eventually pitching the idea of you writing a regular column for them.

Writing a regular column about your area of expertise in the appropriate media gives you credibility, builds your expert image, and can provide great awareness.

You may not want to write a regular column, but perhaps just an occasional article. Some publications publish articles sent to them, so if there are any such in your industry, check them out and submit an article. You will usually find a section on their website with information for people interested in writing for them. If not, find information about the editors and contact them directly.

Social Media

I don't expect I need to tell you what social media is. Social media is everywhere, and it is safe to say that there is not a business that cannot benefit from at least one social media platform in their marketing. But which ones should you be using, and where and how do they fit into the lead management system?

We will be going over the main social media sites, the objective being that you find those that are useful to you and see how you can use them within your marketing program. Social media marketing in and of itself is a huge topic—hey, Facebook marketing on its own is a huge topic—so I will only be able to skim the surface in this book. The idea is to point you in the right direction.

In the reader resources at thoranna.is/mcureader, you will find additional materials and resources about social media. Also, do join the *Marketing Untangled* Facebook group at facebook.com/groups/MarketingUntangledSeries, where you can ask questions and participate in discussions. I pop in regularly, and you will also find that there are other people participating who can share their knowledge and experience.

Social media and content marketing are closely tied together. Social media helps content marketing enormously, and you can't really do social media marketing without content marketing. What would you share if you don't have content?

You need to carefully consider where your target groups' interests lie and why they would want to hang out with you on social media. This is *social* media, and not many people want to be social with someone unless they are getting something out of it.

Another aspect of social media is advertising (PPC), and social media advertising can be very powerful, focused and give a great return on investment—*if* you know how to use it. ;) Just as with any other form of advertising, it is easy to throw money down the drain if you don't know what you are doing.

Marketing is about forming a connection, building a relationship, and by their very nature, that is what social media is about. They are about connections and dialogue—interactivity. They are not a one-sided broadcast medium in the same way as TV, radio, or press.

On social media you have to give before you take. The power lies with the people. They choose whether they want to join you and hang out with you. They can voice their opinions and create a dialogue. Social media is also a great way for people to share things with others, so if you do a good job, you potentially have an enormous amount of people helping you get your product or service out there.

Social media gives you the possibility of building a very strong relationship, but people will go as quickly as they came, and they will not bother to stick around if they don't like what they see and hear. You have to make it worth their while to hang out with you. Content marketing doesn't get much purer than that!

When choosing social media for your marketing program, just as with any other marketing activities, there are a few things you need to keep in mind:

Is your target group there, and is it active? You will find resources at thoranna.is/mcureader to help you determine where your target audience lives on social media.

Do you have the time to do social media marketing properly? If not, don't! The truth is, though, that you can't avoid social media altogether, so you do need to make time for it. However, you don't have to be on every platform. Find one or two that are well aligned with your target audience and brand and focus on those. You may want to set up profiles on others, even just to own the profile name and URL, and then simply put up a notice, in case people find you, to direct people to the profiles where you are active.

Is it the right medium for you? Your target group might be on Twitter, but if you can't stand Twitter, find it too complicated, and are not in any way interested in getting to grips with it, you are never going to use it effectively. Each medium has its own character, and if you, or the person within your business who is going to be managing that medium, don't like it, you have a problem. This will show in your interaction on social media, so you may want to look at alternatives.

Where and how are you planning to use social media within your lead management system? You have to consider this for each of the media you are planning to be on and everything you do on them. Some networks are better for awareness, while others are better for interacting with leads later in the marketing process or may even be best for continuing your relationship with your current customers. Different features within each social media platform are also suitable for different roles in the lead management system. Facebook ads, Facebook stories, Facebook groups and Facebook Messenger are examples of different features of one platform that can be used in different ways, depending on what you want them to do.

How are you going to use social media with your other marketing activities? What do you want people to do? Where are people going to come from to your social media? What do you want them to do as a result of having interacted with you on social media? How are you going to move them from social media to your own channels (email, website, etc.), and how are you going to get the sale?

What do you want to get out of your social media activities? You need to be aware of the different goals you have with your social media. Social media can serve your business in four main ways:

- A key component is to use social media to **listen** to your market and your customers. This can build relationships, build your reputation, and give you valuable information.

- **Influencing** is another goal with social media, i.e., you want to reach more people and get them to interact with you and ultimately buy from you.

- Then there is **networking**, not just with your prospects and customers, but with others that can help you get more awareness in the market and more sales. This could be connecting with influencers, media, or even forming business partnerships.

- Finally, there is **social selling**, i.e., the activities that clinch the deal. Interestingly, though, any social media marketing expert will tell you that you don't sell *on* social media—at least not directly. Social media will not work if you expect it to take people straight from "hi" to the checkout; but if you have already put in the work to lead people through the marketing process, social media can help lead them there.

One quick note before we get into each of the main social media platforms: I have not included any numbers or data in this book. That information would be outdated before I even finished the manuscript, let alone got the book out! If, for example, I put in the number of Facebook users when I am writing this, it will most definitely have changed by the time you read this! ;)

I have also not discussed specific tools or tactics, as this is something that also keeps changing. As an example, a while back, Facebook Live was killing it as a marketing tactic. It got major organic visibility. However, as I am writing this, Facebook has put it firmly on the map and has reduced organic visibility as Live has established itself. Things change fast and, again, if I go into too much detail on tactics, this book will be obsolete before it comes out! :)

Facebook

As I write this, Facebook is the giant in the social media marketing space, has been for a long time, and doesn't seem to be going away any time soon (although someone always seems to be predicting its demise). Generally, for most B2C businesses, it makes sense to be on Facebook. This is not a hard and fast rule, though, and you will need to look at how well this applies in your market and be absolutely sure that your target groups are there.

If you operate in a B2B market, you need to examine more carefully whether Facebook is the right place for you to be. It may well be, but it is not a given. Are your target groups there? Do you have things that you can say and do that suit Facebook as a medium? Facebook is a fairly informal medium, so if your brand is not suited to that, Facebook may not necessarily be the right medium for you. However, don't discount it—check out and test it. That's one of the beauties of online marketing; it's fairly easy and inexpensive to test what works, which is much better than hunches and guesswork. ;) I worked with a cyber security company in a B2B market where Facebook ads worked wonders, against all expectations.

A thing to note about Facebook today is that it is no longer a medium you can get much out of for free. For a long time, it was the small business's dream of a powerful free marketing medium. No more. And that really shouldn't surprise anyone. There is no such thing as a free lunch. ;)

Typically, I recommend my clients have an active Facebook page and get likes for social proof and to show what their brand is all about.

Express your brand—it can help you get found online, as well. But do not to expect to get free organic visibility that will get you anywhere (if it does, consider it a bonus). Sure, you can get organic reach, but you will be spending a lot of time testing and analysing the content that works. That may not require cash, but it requires time, and time is money. You might be better off just spending the money on paid Facebook advertising that may be able to guarantee you better results.

Your Facebook page, however, can come with great insights into your audience—and the ability to use Facebook audience insights, as well. As this is written, Facebook ads are a very effective way of advertising and can give a great return on investment if you know how to use them. However, as with any other advertising medium, it is also very easy to waste money if you don't know what you are doing. It should be noted, too, that indications are that Facebook ads are becoming more and more expensive.

This is a book about marketing communications, not just Facebook, and as previously stated, a printed book about Facebook would be out of date before we know it. But in the reader resources at thoranna.is/mcureader, you'll find links to some great online resources about Facebook for marketing and advertising. You can also ask questions in the *Marketing Untangled* Facebook group at facebook.com/MarketingUntangledSeries. I will answer, as I am sure a lot of others will, as well. :)

Instagram

Instagram has been going from strength to strength for a number of years now and is one of the major players in social media. It is owned by Facebook, so there are also interlinks between the two which strengthen both media, particularly when it comes to advertising and ad targeting.

As always, you need to consider whether your target group is there and also whether you have something to offer a medium like Instagram. It is completely visual, whether through still images or videos, so it lends itself well to products and services that provide ample visual opportunities.

Part of the Instagram culture are Instagram celebrities, which can be a very powerful tool in your influencer marketing. This is also a medium where hashtags rule (Twitter being the other major hashtag medium), so you need to make sure you know how to use them effectively.

Instagram works well with other social media such as Facebook and Twitter, and it is a mobile medium, primarily designed for use on your smartphone.

LinkedIn

LinkedIn is a professional social medium. It is probably the largest online business network and keeps on growing. This is not a medium to share your baby's pictures or photos from your night out on the town. ;) This is a great medium to build your professional brand and your reputation as an expert in your field and to grow and nurture your network through your personal profile.

LinkedIn also offers Company Pages where you can build the image and visibility of your business, as well as groups and an ad platform.

Should you be on LinkedIn? The simple answer: Yes.

I always recommend that you build at least your personal profile on LinkedIn. This helps build your business network, and you know how important your network is to your business.

Whether you should have a Company Page is something that needs to be determined for each business.

In a way, you could say that your personal LinkedIn profile is your CV on steroids. If you would put everything on your CV or the "About" page on your website, people would think you are a bit full of yourself.

On LinkedIn, however, it is perfectly acceptable to put absolutely everything you have done, which makes it a great opportunity to really show people what you've got and why you are the person or company they should do business with. This is particularly strong if selling any type of expert services and a great way to build trust, authority, and credibility.

Use of LinkedIn differs greatly between industries. It is, however, fairly simple to see if the people you want to reach are on there. Just get on there and look for them. If they are there, you should be.

If you are in a B2C market, you might not get to your end consumers on LinkedIn, but you can build your network of collaborators, retailers, and other intermediaries. If you are in a B2B market, chances are you can reach your audience there.

On LinkedIn, you can reach decision makers. This is where you can reach business executives and people with above average income and education.

LinkedIn can be a very powerful marketing medium for SMBs. It is rarely used to its full potential, but it can be a way to reach good customers, build a strong business network, and build your personal brand.

LinkedIn groups are not just a great way to build your network, but they are also a way to keep your finger on the pulse of your industry. Setting up your own LinkedIn group can also be an effective marketing tool.

Pinterest

Various sources cite research that says Pinterest users spend more online, buy more things online, and overall do more shopping online than the users of other social media. At some points in time, sources have claimed that Pinterest has been one of the best social mediums to generate website traffic and that it delivers highest revenue per click than other social mediums. This changes fast, but it is safe to say that for certain industries and target groups, Pinterest can be a powerful marketing tool. At the time of this writing, it is considerably smaller than Facebook, Instagram, Twitter, or LinkedIn, but it has a fairly specific user profile and is strong in the US market.

A visual medium, Pinterest works particularly well for visually rich businesses, such as in fashion, design, arts and crafts, beauty and health. You'd be surprised though at the kinds of businesses that can do well on Pinterest, given a little visual creativity. Infographics, images, and graphics with text and all sorts of instructional graphics do great on there, as well.

As I was teaching about social media marketing, one of my students challenged me, saying that there was no way there was anything on Pinterest for guys. So, we put it to the test and did a search for "fly fishing." To the student's amazement, there was a treasure trove of great stuff on fly fishing on Pinterest, and he quickly signed up and started building his boards related to fishing. See, assuming only makes an ASS-of-U-and-ME, and in the online world, you can generally find things out reliably and quickly, removing your need for guesswork. ;)

Pinterest users are browsing—window shopping—and are, therefore, often ready to buy. In comparison, Facebook is like a party which you are crashing when trying to promote your stuff. A not uncommon Pinterest journey would be browsing through fashion pins, spotting a gorgeous top, clicking to view it, clicking to view it better, and then you're on the product page and "oops, I just bought it!" ;) ... that doesn't happen so much on other social media.

Pinterest keeps developing its paid marketing tools, offering some very interesting possibilities. However, at the time of this writing, they are available to businesses in only a few major English-speaking countries.

Pinterest can be a brilliant marketing tool, particularly if you sell products online. As with any other social medium, though, you need to be sure that your target group is there, and you know how to get the most out of the medium.

SlideShare

SlideShare has been called YouTube for PowerPoint presentations. It can be a very effective content marketing tool, particularly for B2B markets. It also integrates well with its owner, LinkedIn.

SlideShare not only provides an alternative format for your content marketing, but through good search-optimised content, it can also be used to gain awareness, drive traffic to your blog or website, and get people to subscribe to your mailing list.

Snapchat

Snapchat can't be left out of any list of major social media to use for marketing, although they've had a bumpy ride. People had great expectations when the company went public, but they haven't really been able to live up to them, most notably by not being able to monetise the platform through advertising to the extent that the market expected.

Another visual medium, it skews toward a younger audience, although this may have changed by the time you read this! :D (Interestingly, in my native Iceland, the age distribution is quite different, with a lot of middle-aged people on Snapchat—it just goes to show you that you have to know *your* market. ;))

Snapchat is less viral in nature than most of the other main social media platforms, which means you have to work hard to promote it. Another drawback of using Snapchat for marketing is that it is very much a live medium, whereas with many of the other social media, you can schedule updates using third-party social media management tools (and natively on Facebook and Instagram), you can't do this for

Snapchat. This makes it an even more time-consuming medium than most, and social media is time consuming already.

For businesses whose target audience is on Snapchat and who have a brand image that fits the medium, it can be a good marketing tool. However you need to make sure you have the resources, i.e. time, to spend on it, in order to get results. Every social media platform has their own culture, and Snapchat has a very particular one, so it is also crucial that whoever is managing your Snapchat fully understands it.

Twitter

You no doubt have heard very divided opinions when it comes to Twitter. Some love it, others hate it, many do not understand it. If your target group is there and you are ready to do the work, Twitter can be a powerful marketing tool. However, if your target audience isn't there, there is no reason for you to be there, and if you are not ready to do the work, you may as well skip it.

Sure, a tweet may only be 140 characters, but to get results on Twitter, you need to be all in. A quick scan at the time of writing shows Buffer saying you should tweet 14 times per day, Coschedule says 15, FastCompany says between 5 and 30, and others have said as much as 40 or 50! See, this is what I mean by all in. Not only do you have to tweet quite a bit, but to know what the magic frequency number is for you, you need to test and measure. And this is just one part. There are a lot of other things you need to do to get results on Twitter, including mastering those hashtags (on Instagram, you can pretty much use as many hashtags as you want, whereas on Twitter there supposedly is a magic number of 2-3 per tweet, and it matters where they are in the tweet—oh, and, of course, what hashtags they are).

If you are ready to tame the beast and your audience is there, you can get a lot out of Twitter for your marketing and your networking, and it is very useful to keep your ear to the ground and finger on the pulse. In certain industries, Twitter is not optional, but instead considered to be mandatory, and in many industries, there is an expectation that you provide customer service there. You could also decide just to use Twitter for networking with bloggers, media, or influencers in your industry, but not so much for general marketing.

As always, it is a question of knowing whether your peeps are there. Finding that out is definitely task number one. If you have analysed your target groups properly, you would know whether they are on Twitter or not. If you haven't, go check out *Target Groups Untangled*—you will find all about it in the reader resources, which you can access at thoranna.is/mcureader.

Tumblr

Tumblr has been called part microblogging and part social networking. It's a blog, but it has a lot of features that you'll be familiar with from social networks. It is generally considered to have a strong community, although at the time of writing this, it has experienced a decline. On Tumblr, people share content, follow others, and reblog in the same way as we know from many other social mediums.

It is very simple to set up a blog on Tumblr, but it won't give you as many possibilities as large blogging systems like WordPress. The audience tends to be in the younger categories, and Tumblr is generally quite a visual medium. As an example, you will find a lot of fashion blogs on there.

If your target audience is on Tumblr, you will want to be there. If it isn't and you are just choosing a blogging platform, you will want to consider which platform to use in the context of other things, such as your main website content management system (CMS), search engine optimisation, and such.

YouTube

YouTube should need no introduction. The video platform has been a strong online presence since its birth in 2005. Videos can be a powerful marketing tool; and if you know how to use it effectively, so can You-Tube. For a long time, YouTube has been the second largest online search engine after Google, and as I'm writing this, it has over a billion users! So, I think it's safe to say it offers some benefits as a marketing tool.

Getting a lot out of YouTube as a social medium can be quite hard work, though, so you need to be sure you are up for it before using it as such. If, however, you just want to use videos in marketing, you will want to use YouTube, even if only to have your (free) branded YouTube channel as a central place for your videos from where they can spread far and wide.

YouTube has been said to have a somewhat special relationship with search engines, particularly its owner, Google. Search engine optimised YouTube videos have a very good chance of getting high search rankings.

You can use YouTube to get traffic to your website, where you can continue the lead management process. Remember that videos on You-Tube can also be a great part of your content marketing strategy.

More Social Media

There is no way I can list all the social media options available, so I've only mentioned the main ones in the Western world. The key is to know your market and target groups and know where your audience is.

In addition to the main ones discussed here, there are also social media sites for specific niches, such as Behance for graphic design and Ravelry for knitters. Certain countries and geographic areas have social media sites that are huge there but are unknown elsewhere, such as QZone in China, VK in Russia, and Taringa in Latin America. As I'm writing this, a wealth of articles say TikTok will be the next big thing. I decided to leave it out – I also remember when Periscope was to be the next big thing, and Vine and …

The term "social media" also applies to a lot of platforms that we would perhaps not consider viable marketing tools. Platforms such as WhatsApp and Skype are more pure communication tools in nature and don't have the mass media aspects of say Facebook or YouTube. Others have more of a good old forum flavour, such as Quora and Reddit, and yet others are designed more for content discovery, such as Digg and AllTop.

The key is to find the right platforms for your business and learn to use them effectively. As always, knowledge of your market and audience is of utmost importance.

Social Media Management Tools

Around social media, a whole ecosystem of tools has developed to help manage social media and measure results. Here are some of the things that social media management tools can help you with (please note, different solutions may have different combinations of these features):

- Post to all (or most) of your social media profiles from one place
- Schedule your social media posts
- Measure the return on investment of your social media efforts through analytics
- Track mentions, to help you manage your online reputation
- Manage social conversations
- Recommend content for you to post (content curation)
- And more tools and more features of those tools continue to come out

To see which social media tools may best suit you, here are a few you may want to check out. Also, try a Google search for "social media management tools."

- Buffer.com
- Hootsuite.com
- PostPlanner.com
- SproutSocial.com
- MeetEdgar.com
- Tweetdeck.com (for Twitter only)
- Later.com

Building Your Marketing Communications Program

I have covered a lot in this book, yet there is so much I still want to tell you. I hope I have given you an understanding of how your marketing activities need to work together as a system to get the most out of them, and I've introduced you to some of the components you can use to build your marketing communications program. I have given you the essential recipe and a wealth of ingredients to choose from so you can serve up the right fare for your people. Now it's up to you to get into that marketing kitchen and start cooking.

By now, you know that you need to choose the marketing activities that can best reach your audience and build your brand. You also need to be sure you are choosing marketing activities that work for you and your team and you have the right resources, skills, and mindset for what you are going to include in your marketing program. And you need to ensure that the activities in your program lead people through the marketing process from awareness and interest to liking and trusting you, trying you out in some way, and then to the sale—but not just one sale—you want to build an ongoing relationship that leads to repeat business. What are you going to use to get attention and gain interest, i.e., what are your lead generators? How are you going to capture those leads so you can more effectively nurture your relationship with them and get them to like and trust you? How are you going to let them try your product or service? How are you going to give them that nudge necessary to get them to open their wallets and make the purchase?

What are you going to do to get repeat sales, and how are you going to encourage those referrals?

In order to move people through that marketing process, you will build your lead management system. You will select activities that generate those all-important leads by creating awareness and getting them interested. These are the activities that get you out there in front of a cold audience that has never seen you before, things such as advertising, SEO, content marketing, social media, and such.

Then you want to capture those leads to ensure that you can continue the conversation and build that relationship without having to pay through the nose each and every time. Using great content, lead magnets, and landing pages will be your strongest way to capture them, although building your followers on social media also helps to lower that cost of contact.

Once you have captured the lead, the relationship building continues with nurturing. Emails are, at the time of this writing and have been for a considerable time, the strongest lead nurture tool available, and there is no indication that this will change any time soon. But email marketing also requires good quality content, so make sure you have something to email them about other than just "buy from me." Don't ever forget the analogy of the dating process... if you don't take time to get to know them and let them get to know you, your chances of getting a yes to that proposal are significantly reduced—you might even get a slap in the face.

Remember to have a clear goal with everything you do in your marketing and to measure whether things are working. You don't have time and money to waste. Your marketing needs to work, but if you don't measure it, you'll have no way of knowing whether it does.

Remember that this process takes time, and no matter how fantastic your product or service is and how much you know that people need it, people will also need that extra nudge to take action. Make sure you use the tactics available to you to encourage them and ensure that the transaction process is as smooth as possible.

Below you can see a simple visual diagram of a marketing program. You may find it useful, you might not, but hopefully it will help you get a better grasp of how you can structure your marketing program. In my work in lots of different businesses in varied industries, I have found that the programs tend to be fairly similar. The greatest variation is usually in the first stage, the lead generation phase, where you want to get awareness and interest, as can be expected with different target groups that are accessible in different places and mediums. As you move further, for most businesses, I recommend you move to capturing the lead to your email list and do most of your lead nurturing there.

The main differentiation between businesses lies in the choice of target audiences and how you differentiate yourself through your brand and message. The marketing activities are merely a vehicle to reach that target audience and convey that brand and, therefore, do not really provide a source of differentiation beyond that. Everyone can learn the technical ins and outs of using Facebook, email marketing software, or uploading a video to YouTube, but it is the substance that matters.

If you want to improve your understanding of your target groups, or build a stronger and more powerful brand, you may want to check out other books in the *Marketing Untangled* Series. You will find information in the reader resources at thoranna.is/mcureader.

In the reader resources at thoranna.is/mcureader, you will find additional materials and resources. I also want to encourage you to join the *Marketing Untangled* Facebook group at facebook.com/groups/MarketingUntangledSeries, where you can ask questions and participate in discussions. I pop in regularly, and you will also find that there are other people in there who can share their knowledge and experience.

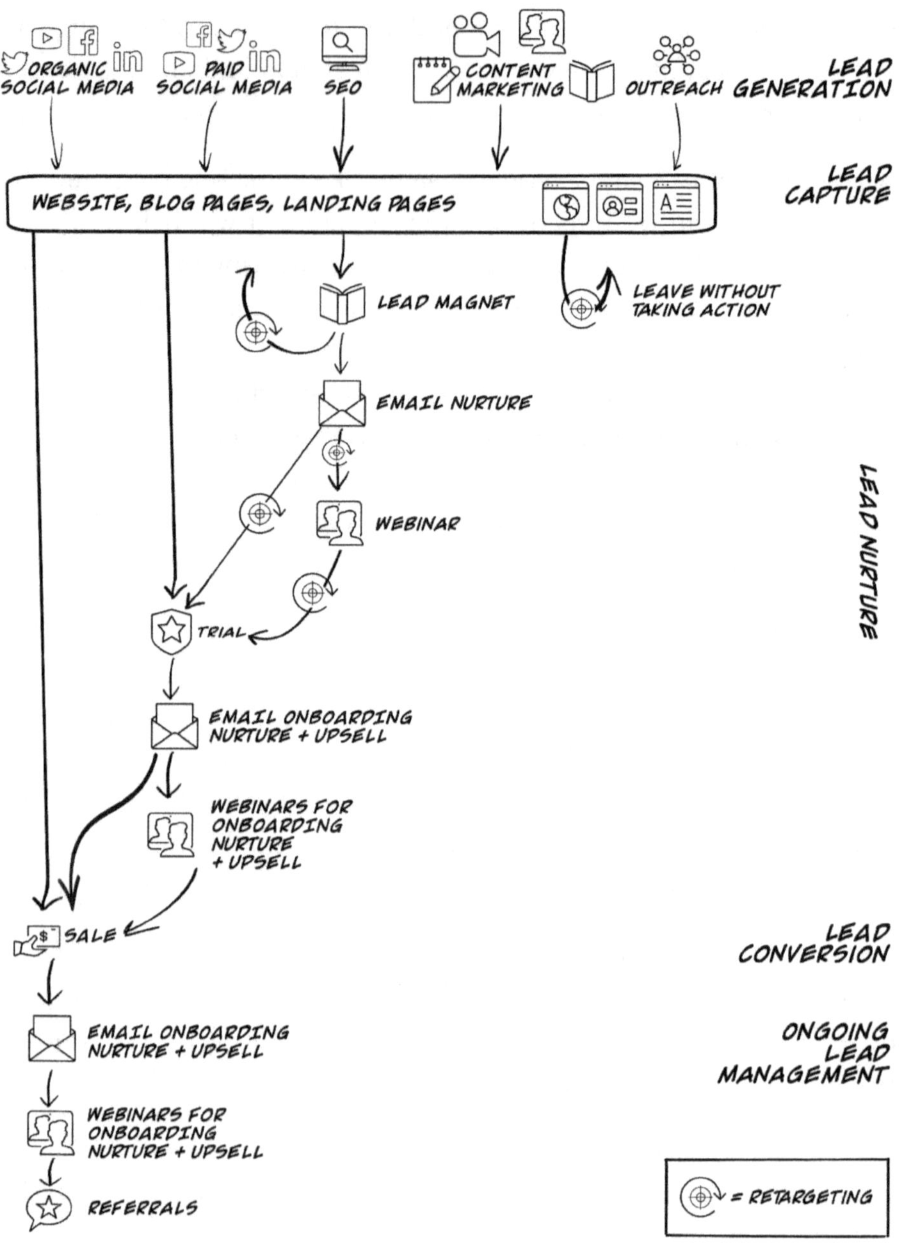
ORGANIC SOCIAL MEDIA
PAID SOCIAL MEDIA
SEO
CONTENT MARKETING
OUTREACH
LEAD GENERATION
WEBSITE, BLOG PAGES, LANDING PAGES
LEAD CAPTURE
LEAD MAGNET
LEAVE WITHOUT TAKING ACTION
EMAIL NURTURE
WEBINAR
LEAD NURTURE
TRIAL
EMAIL ONBOARDING NURTURE + UPSELL
WEBINARS FOR ONBOARDING NURTURE + UPSELL
SALE
LEAD CONVERSION
EMAIL ONBOARDING NURTURE + UPSELL
ONGOING LEAD MANAGEMENT
WEBINARS FOR ONBOARDING NURTURE + UPSELL
REFERRALS
= RETARGETING

For now, I'll just say I hope you've found this useful and I've managed to get all this information across in a manner you can understand. There is so much more I would love to tell you, but that is for another time, perhaps another book, or who knows, by working together! By using what I have taught you in this book, you are on your way to more effective marketing and a more successful business. I would love to hear about your success, so don't hesitate to drop me a line—you'll find a list of my social profiles below.

I'm not going to say, "good luck," because it has nothing to do with luck. It has everything to do with your hard work—you reap what you sow. May you reap generously.

All the best,
Thoranna

P.S. This is not an academic book. It is designed to be accessible to non-marketing specialists and non-academics and a practical guide on *doing* for those who may know the theory but lack tools and tactics in the trenches. Therefore, you won't see the text broken up with brackets and names and all those things you would expect in textbooks and journal articles. Many tend to find them distracting, and it would also take away from the accessible tone of the book.

The book is, however, firmly based both in academic research and practical knowledge and experience, including mine and that of other warriors in the marketing trenches. Below you will find references, both ones that are mentioned in the text, but also some not mentioned specifically but which have contributed to my knowledge and experience on the subject of marketing communications.

On thoranna.is/booksandresources, you can also find more information about books and resources which underpin my writing and my work in various areas of marketing and branding. I encourage you to check them out to learn more and open up your marketing world. ;)

About the Author

Thoranna is a marketing specialist with wide-ranging experience dating back to the beginning of the century. (Ehm, although she is not ancient! ;) A self-confessed marketing nerd, she views marketing not just as her job, but also a passion—for her, it combines the right and left brain, bringing together business and creativity. Marketing also resonates with her as an actress and performer because it is centred around communicating with and influencing people.

Thoranna has worked with global advertising agencies Publicis and McCann Erickson, as well as within the finance and tech industries—particularly with SaaS products. She has worked with a wide spectrum of consulting clients, ranging from health companies, baby products, charities, tourism, photography, web services, construction, education, coaching, tech, non-profit, and more. She holds an MBA with Distinction, focused on strategic marketing, from the University of Westminster in London. She is also a certified digital marketing specialist through DigitalMarketer's extensive training programs.

Soon after the economic collapse of 2008, Thoranna started working with entrepreneurs and start-ups and has been very involved in her local start-up and innovation scene—consulting, mentoring, and teaching. Her passion for marketing and entrepreneurship, extensive speaking experience, and media appearances give her a unique perspective on providing jargon-free, practical marketing advice. Thoranna is not a fan of putting on airs and shrouding herself in incomprehensible jargon to show her expertise but believes in clear communication. With her, what you see is what you get.

Thoranna lives in Iceland with her husband and two children. Before starting her career in marketing, she trained for musical theatre, subsequently working as an actress and singer. Being too straight for the Bohemian life (and today probably too wild for the business world ;), she appeared on television and toured the United Kingdom with the Rocky Horror Show—even meeting the legendary Richard O'Brian. Then, she did a 180-degree turn toward the business world. Thoranna is constantly amazed at how much her former life helps her and those she works with in business!

Find out more at thoranna.is and on social media:

Facebook.com/thoranna.is
Twitter.com/thoranna
LinkedIn.com/in/thorannakristin
Pinterest.com/thoranna
Instagram.com/thorannamarketing

Endnotes

[1] Al Ries & Laura Ries, *The 22 Immutable Laws of Branding. How to Build a Product or Service into a World-Class Brand*, Collins Business, 2002

[2] Peter Drucker, *The Practice of Management*. Harper Business, 2010.

[3] Friðrik Eysteinsson and Þórhallur Örn Guðlaugsson, 2012. Literature review at University of Iceland. Presentation by Friðrik for Dokkan in February 2012, *Hvers vegna ná sum fyrirtæki viðvarandi betri árangri en önnur?* Or: *Why do some companies consistently perform better than others?* http://www.slideshare.net/Dokkan/fridrik-eisteins-feb2012.

[4] Peter Drucker, *The Practice of Management*. Harper Business, 2010.

[5] Maureen Farrell, *How to Market Your New Idea*, Forbes, 20017: https://www.forbes.com/2007/12/21/marketing-branding-identity-ent-cx_mf_1221brand.html#33feaf976a0a

[6] Seth Godin, *Purple Cow: Transform Your Business by Being Remarkable*, Penguin Books, 2002

[7] Girls Don't Poop – PooPourri.com: https://youtu.be/ZKLnhuzh9uY PooPourri.com accessed in 2013

[8] PooPourri.com, 2013

[9] Peter Drucker, *The Essential Drucker*, Butterworth-Heineman 2001

[10] *B2B's Digital Evolution*, CEB's Marketing Leadership Council, Think with Google, February 2013: https://www.thinkwithgoogle.com/marketing-resources/b2b-digital-evolution/ Meghan Heuer, *Three Myths of the "67 Percent" Statistic*, Forrester / SiriusDecisions, July 3rd 2013: https://www.siriusdecisions.com/blog/three-myths-of-the-67-percent-statistic

[11] Corina Paraschiv & Olivier L'Haridon, *Loss aversion: origin, components and marketing implications*, Recherche et Applications en Marketing, 2008, Vol.23(2), pp.67-82

12 Thomas Smith, *Successful Advertising*, 1885

13 David Meerman Scott, *The New Rules of Marketing and PR*, Wiley, 2017

14 David A. Aaker, *Managing Brand Equity*, Free Press, 1991

15 Austin McCraw, *This Just Tested: Stock images or real people?*, April 8th 2011: https://marketingexperiments.com/digital-advertising/stock-images-tested

16 Sean Ellis, *Find a Growth Hacker for Your Startup*, 2010: https://www.startup-marketing.com/where-are-all-the-growth-hackers/

17 Oli Gardner, *The unGlossary of A/B Testing: Terminology & Tips to Run Better Tests*, 2012: https://unbounce.com/a-b-testing/glossary/

18 Ryan Deiss, [DOWNLOAD] *9 Lead Magnet Ideas with Examples (And ONE That Generated 35,859 Leads In 60 Days for DigitalMarketer...)*, 2017: https://www.digitalmarketer.com/blog/lead-magnet-ideas-funnel/

19 Malcolm McDonald, *Marketing Plans: How to Prepare Them. How to Use Them*, 5th edition, Butterworth-Heineman, 2002

20 Adam T. Sutton, *Content Marketing: Videos attract 300% more traffic and nurture leads*, Marketing Sherpa, Dec 14th 2011: https://www.marketingsherpa.com/article/how-to/videos-attract-300-more-traffic.

21 Jay Levinson & Jeannie Levinson, *The Best of Guerilla Marketing: Guerilla Marketing Remix*, Entrepreneur Press, 2011

Further References

Although not referred to directly in the endnotes, I would be remiss if I didn't also mention the following books and resources which have influenced my writing, although the list is by no means exhaustive and a lot more should be listed:

Copyblogger, Authority, https://my.copyblogger.com/join-authority/, 2015-2017

David Meerman Scott, *The New Rules of Marketing & PR: How to Use Social Media, Online Video, Mobile Applications, Blogs, New Releases, and Viral Marketing to Reach Buyers Directly*, 4th Edition, Wiley, 2013

DigitalMarketer HQ Mastery and Certification Programs, http://hq.digitalmarketer.com/, 2019

DigitalMarketer Lab, http://lab.digitalmarketer.com/, 2016-2019

Jay Conrad Levinson, *Guerilla Marketing. Easy and Inexpensive Strategies for Making Big Profits from Your Small Business*, Piatkus, 2007

Jeff Walker, *Launch. An Internet Millionaire's Secret Formula to Sell Almost Anything Online, Build a Business You Love, and Live the Life of Your Dreams*, Morgan James Publishing, 2014

John Jantsch, *Duct Tape Marketing Revised and Updated: The World's Most Practical Small Business Marketing Guide*, Thomas Nelson, 2011

Philip Kotler, *Marketing Management*, International Millennium Edition, Prentice Hall, 2000

Robert B. Cialdini, *Influence: The Psychology of Persuasion*, Revised Edition, Harper Business, 2006

Robert B. Cialdini, *Pre-Suasion: A Revolutionary Way to Influence and Persuade*, Simon & Schuster, 2018

Russell Brunson, *Dotcom Secret: The Underground Playbook for Growing Your Company Online...*, Morgan James Publishing, 2015

Ryan Deiss, *Customer Value Optimization: How to Build an Unstoppable Business*, DigitalMarketer Blog, http://www.digitalmarketer.com/customer-value-optimization/, August 20th, 2015

Seth Godin, *Permission Marketing*, Pocket Books, 2007

Various authors, DigitalMarketer Blog, https://www.digitalmarketer.com/blog/